AF553450

METHODS OF FOOD PRESERVATION

By

Dr. Pradeep Shrivastava

Department of Zoology

Vikram University

Ujjain (India)

DISCOVERY PUBLISHING HOUSE PVT. LTD.

NEW DELHI-110 002

First Published - 2013

Reprinted - 2016

ISBN: 978-93-5056-282-6

Methods of Food Preservation

Published by:

DISCOVERY PUBLISHING HOUSE PVT. LTD.
4383/4B, Ansari Road, Darya Ganj
New Delhi-110 002 (India)
Phone: +91-11-23279245, 43596064-65
Fax: +91-11-23253475
E-mail: discoverypublishinghouse@gmail.com
sales@discoverypublishinggroup.com
web: www.discoverypublishinggroup.com

Printed at:
Infinity Imaging Systems
Delhi

Preface

Food preservation is the process of treating and handling food to stop or slow down spoilage (loss of quality, edibility or nutritional value).

Preservation usually involves preventing the growth of bacteria, yeasts, fungi, and other micro-organisms (although some methods work by introducing benign bacteria, or fungi to the food), as well as retarding the oxidation of fats which cause rancidity. Food preservation can also include processes which inhibit visual deterioration that can occur during food preparation; such as the enzymatic browning reaction in apples after they are cut.

Many processes designed to preserve food will involve a number of food preservation methods. Preserving fruit, by turning it into jam, for example, involves boiling (to reduce the fruit's moisture content and to kill bacteria, yeasts, etc.), sugaring (to prevent their re-growth) and sealing within an airtight jar (to prevent recontamination). There are many traditional methods of preserving food that limit the energy inputs and reduce carbon footprint.

Maintaining or creating nutritional value, texture and flavour is an important aspect of food preservation, although, historically, some methods drastically altered the character of the food being preserved. In many cases these changes have now come to be seen as desirable qualities — cheese, yoghurt and pickled onions being common examples.

Some foods, such as many cheeses, wines, and beers will keep for a long time because their production uses specific micro-organisms that combat spoilage from other less benign organisms. These micro-organisms keep pathogens in check by creating an environment toxic for themselves and other micro-organisms by producing acid or alcohol. Starter micro-organisms, salt, hops, controlled (usually cool) temperatures, controlled (usually low) levels of oxygen and/or other methods are used to create the specific controlled conditions that will support the desirable organisms that produce food fit for human consumption.

3D stick model of nisin. Some lactic acid bacteria manufacture nisin. It is a particularly effective preservative.

Biopreservation is the use of natural or controlled microbiota or antimicrobials as a way of preserving food and extending it's shelf life. Beneficial bacteria or the fermentation products produced by these bacteria are used in biopreservation to control spoilage and render pathogens inactive in food. It is a benign ecological approach which is gaining increasing attention.

Of special interest are lactic acid bacteria (LAB). Lactic acid bacteria have antagonistic properties which make them particularly useful as biopreservatives. When LABs compete for nutrients, their metabolites often include active antimicrobials such as lactic and acetic acid, hydrogen peroxide, and peptide bacteriocins. Some LABs produce the antimicrobial nisin which is a particularly effective preservative.

These days LAB bacteriocins are used as an integral part of hurdle technology. Using them in combination with other preservative techniques can effectively control spoilage bacteria and other pathogens, and can inhibiting the activities of a wide spectrum of organisms, including inherently resistant Gram-negative bacteria.

High pressure food preservation refers to high pressure used for food preservation. "Pressed inside a vessel exerting 70,000 pounds per square inch (480 MPa) or more, food can be processed so that it retains its fresh appearance, flavour, texture and nutrients while disabling harmful microorganisms and slowing spoilage". By 2001, adequate commercial equipment was developed so that by 2005 the process was being used for products ranging from orange juice to guacamole to deli meats and widely sold.

—Author

Contents

1 Introduction

Food preservation is the process of treating and handling food to stop or slow down spoilage (loss of quality, edibility or nutritional value).

Preservation usually involves preventing the growth of bacteria, yeasts, fungi, and other micro-organisms (although some methods work by introducing benign bacteria, or fungi to the food), as well as retarding the oxidation of fats which cause rancidity. Food preservation can also include processes which inhibit visual deterioration that can occur during food preparation; such as the enzymatic browning reaction in apples after they are cut.

Many processes designed to preserve food will involve a number of food preservation methods. Preserving fruit, by turning it into jam, for example, involves boiling (to reduce the fruit's moisture content and to kill bacteria, yeasts, etc.), sugaring (to prevent their re-growth) and sealing within an airtight jar (to prevent recontamination). There are many traditional methods of preserving food that limit the energy inputs and reduce carbon footprint.

Maintaining or creating nutritional value, texture and flavour is an important aspect of food preservation, although, historically, some methods drastically altered the character of the food being preserved. In many cases these changes have now come to be seen as desirable qualities — cheese, yoghurt and pickled onions being common examples.

Preservation processes include:

- Heating to kill or denature micro-organisms (*e.g.* boiling)
- Oxidation (*e.g.* use of sulfur dioxide)
- Toxic inhibition (*e.g.* smoking, use of carbon dioxide, vinegar, alcohol etc.)
- Dehydration (drying)
- Osmotic inhibition (*e.g.* use of syrups)
- Low temperature inactivation (*e.g.* freezing)
- Ultra high water pressure (*e.g.* fresherized, a kind of 'cold' pasteurization, the pressure kills naturally occurring pathogens, which cause food deterioration and affect food safety)
- Combinations of these methods

Drying

One of the oldest methods of food preservation is by drying, which reduces water activity sufficiently to prevent or delay bacterial growth.

Refrigeration

Refrigeration preserves food by slowing down the growth and reproduction of micro-organisms and the action of enzymes which cause food to rot. The introduction of commercial and domestic refrigerators drastically improved the diets of many in the Western world by allowing foods such as fresh fruit, salads and dairy products to be stored safely for longer periods, particularly during warm weather.

Freezing

Freezing is also one of the most commonly used processes commercially and domestically for preserving a very wide range of food including prepared food stuffs which would not have required freezing in their unprepared state. For example, potato waffles are stored in the freezer, but potatoes themselves require only a cool dark place to ensure many months' storage. Cold stores provide large volume, long-term storage for strategic food stocks held in case of national emergency in many countries.

Vacuum Packing

Vacuum-packing stores food in a vacuum environment, usually in an air-tight bag or bottle. The vacuum environment strips bacteria of oxygen needed for survival, slowing spoiling. Vacuum-packing is commonly used for storing nuts to reduce loss of flavour from oxidation.

Salting

Salting or curing draws moisture from the meat through a process of osmosis. Meat is cured with salt or sugar, or a combination of the two. Nitrates and nitrites are also often used to cure meat and contribute the characteristic pink colour, as well as inhibition of *Clostridium botulinum*.

Sugaring

Sugar is used to preserve fruits, either in syrup with fruit such as apples, pears, peaches, apricots, plums or in crystallized form where the preserved material is cooked in sugar to the point of crystallisation and the resultant product is then stored dry. This method is used for the skins of citrus fruit (candied peel), angelica and ginger. A modification of this process produces glacé fruit such as glacé cherries where the fruit is preserved in sugar but is then extracted from the syrup and sold, the preservation being maintained by the sugar content of the fruit and the superficial coating of syrup. The use of sugar is often combined with alcohol for preservation of luxury products such as fruit in brandy or other spirits. These should not be confused with fruit flavoured spirits such as cherry brandy or Sloe gin.

Artificial Food Additives

Preservative food additives can be *antimicrobial*; which inhibit the growth of bacteria or fungi, including mold, or *antioxidant*; such as oxygen absorbers, which inhibit the oxidation of food constituents.

Common antimicrobial preservatives include calcium propionate, sodium nitrate, sodium nitrite, sulfites (sulfur dioxide, sodium bisulfite, potassium hydrogen sulfite, etc.) and disodium EDTA. Antioxidants include BHA and BHT. Other preservatives include formaldehyde (usually in solution), glutaraldehyde (kills insects), ethanol and methylchloroisothiazolinone.

Pickling

Pickling is a method of preserving food in an edible anti-microbial liquid. Pickling can be broadly categorized as chemical pickling for example, In chemical pickling, the food is placed in an edible liquid that inhibits or kills bacteria and other micro-organisms. Typical pickling agents include brine (high in salt), vinegar, alcohol, and vegetable oil, especially olive oil but also many other oils. Many chemical pickling processes also involve heating or boiling so that the food being preserved becomes saturated with the pickling agent. Common chemically pickled foods include cucumbers, peppers, corned beef, herring, and eggs, as well mixed vegetables such as piccalilli.

In fermentation pickling, the food itself produces the preservation agent, typically by a process that produces lactic acid. Fermented pickles include sauerkraut, nukazuke, kimchi, surströmming, and curtido. Some pickled cucumbers are also fermented.

In commercial pickles, a preservative like sodium benzoate or EDTA may also be added to enhance shelf life.

Lye

Sodium hydroxide (lye) makes food too alkaline for bacterial growth. Lye will saponify fats in the food, which will change its flavour and texture. Lutefisk uses lye in its preparation, as do some olive recipes. Modern recipes for century eggs also call for lye. Masa harina and hominy use agricultural lime in their preparation and this is often misheard as 'lye'.

Canning and Bottling

Canning involves cooking food, sealing it in sterile cans or jars, and boiling the containers to kill or weaken any remaining bacteria as a form of sterilization. It was invented by Nicolas Appert. Foods have varying degrees of natural protection against spoilage and may require that the final step occur in a pressure cooker. High-acid fruits like strawberries require no preservatives to can and only a short boiling cycle, whereas marginal fruits such as tomatoes require longer boiling and addition of other acidic elements. Low acid foods, such as vegetables and meats require pressure canning. Food preserved by canning or bottling is at immediate risk of spoilage once the can or bottle has been opened.

Lack of quality control in the canning process may allow ingress of water or micro-organisms. Most such failures are rapidly detected as decomposition within the can causes gas production and the can will swell or burst. However, there have been examples of poor manufacture (underprocessing) and poor hygiene allowing contamination of canned food by the obligate anaerobe *Clostridium botulinum*, which produces an acute toxin within the food, leading to severe illness or death. This organism produces no gas or obvious taste and remains undetected by taste or smell. Its toxin is denatured by cooking, though. Cooked mushrooms, handled poorly and then canned, can support the growth of Staphylococcus aureus, which produces a toxin that is not destroyed by canning or subsequent reheating.

Jellying

Food may be preserved by cooking in a material that solidifies to form a gel. Such materials include gelatine, agar, maize flour and arrowroot flour. Some foods naturally form a protein gel when cooked such as eels and elvers, and sipunculid worms which are a delicacy in the town of Xiamen in Fujian province of the People's Republic of China. Jellied eels are a delicacy in the East End of London where they are eaten with mashed potatoes. Potted meats in aspic, (a gel made from gelatine and clarified meat broth) were a common way of serving meat off-cuts in the UK until the 1950s. Many jugged meats are also jellied.

Potting

A traditional British way of preserving meat (particularly shrimp) is by setting it in a pot and sealing it with a layer of fat. Also common is potted chicken liver; compare pâté.

Jugging

Meat can be preserved by jugging, the process of stewing the meat (commonly game or fish) in a covered earthenware jug or casserole. The animal to be jugged is usually cut into pieces, placed into a tightly-sealed jug with brine or gravy, and stewed. Red wine and/or the animal's own blood is sometimes added to the cooking liquid. Jugging was a popular method of preserving meat up until the middle of the 20th century.

Irradiation

Irradiation of food is the exposure of food to ionizing radiation; either high-energy electrons or X-rays from accelerators, or by gamma rays (emitted from radioactive sources as Cobalt-60 or Caesium-137). The treatment has a range of effects, including killing bacteria, molds and insect pests, reducing the ripening and spoiling of fruits, and at higher doses inducing sterility. The technology may be compared to pasteurization; it is sometimes called 'cold pasteurization', as the product is not heated. Irradiation is not effective against viruses or prions, it cannot eliminate toxins already formed by microorganisms, and is only useful for food of high initial quality.

The radiation process is unrelated to nuclear energy, but it may use the radiation emitted from radioactive nuclides produced in nuclear reactors. Ionizing radiation is hazardous to life (hence its usefulness in sterilisation); for this reason irradiation facilities have a heavily shielded irradiation room where the process takes place. Radiation safety procedures ensure that neither the workers in such facility nor the environment receive any radiation dose from the facility. Irradiated food does not become radioactive, and national and international expert bodies have declared food irradiation as wholesome. However, the wholesomeness of consuming such food is disputed by opponents and consumer organizations. National and international expert bodies have declared food irradiation as 'wholesome'; UN-organizations as WHO and FAO are endorsing to use food irradiation. International legislation on whether food may be irradiated or not varies worldwide from no regulation to full banning. Irradiation may allow lower quality or contaminated foodstuffs to be rendered marketable.

It is estimated that about 500,000 tons of food items are irradiated per year worldwide in over 40 countries. These are mainly spices and condiments with an increasing segment of fresh fruit irradiated for fruit fly quarantine.

Pulsed Electric Field Processing

Pulsed electric field (PEF) processing is a method for processing cells by means of brief pulses of a strong electric field. PEF holds potential as a type of low temperature alternative pasteurization process for sterilizing food products. In PEF processing, a substance is placed between two electrodes, then the pulsed electric field is applied. The electric field enlarges the pores of the cell membranes which kills the cells and releases their contents. PEF for food processing is a developing technology still being researched. There have been limited industrial applications of PEF processing for the pasteurization of fruit juices.

Modified Atmosphere

Modifying atmosphere is a way to preserve food by operating on the atmosphere around it. Salad crops which are notoriously difficult to preserve are now being packaged in sealed bags with an atmosphere modified to reduce the oxygen (O_2) concentration and increase the carbon dioxide

(CO_2) concentration. There is concern that although salad vegetables retain their appearance and texture in such conditions, this method of preservation may not retain nutrients, especially vitamins. Grains may be preserved using carbon dioxide by one of two methods; either using a block of dry ice placed in the bottom and the can is filled with grain or the container can be purged from the bottom by gaseous carbon dioxide from a cylinder or bulk supply vessel.

Carbon dioxide prevents insects, and depending on concentration, mold, and oxidation from damaging the grain. Grain stored in this way can remain edible for five years.

Nitrogen gas (N_2) at concentrations of 98 per cent or higher is also used effectively to kill insects in grain through hypoxia. However, carbon dioxide has an advantage in this respect as it kills organisms through hypercarbia and depending on concentration hypoxia and, requiring concentrations of above 35 per cent , or so. This makes carbon dioxide preferable for fumigation in situations where a hermetic seal cannot be maintained.

Burial in the Ground

Burial of food can preserve it due to a variety of factors: lack of light, lack of oxygen, cool temperatures, pH level, or desiccants in the soil. Burial may be combined with other methods such as salting or fermentation.

Many root vegetables are very resistant to spoilage and require no other preservation than storage in cool dark conditions, for example by burial in the ground, such as in a storage clamp.

Century eggs are created by placing eggs in alkaline mud (or other alkaline substance) resulting in their 'inorganic' fermentation through raised pH instead of spoiling. The fermentation preserves them and breaks down some of the complex, less flavourful proteins and fats into simpler more flavourful ones.

Most foods can be preserved in soil that is very dry and salty (thus a desiccant), or soil that is frozen.

Cabbage was traditionally buried in the fall in northern farms in the USA for preservation. Some methods keep it crispy while other methods produce sauerkraut . A similar process is used in the traditional production of kimchi.

Sometimes meat is buried under conditions which cause preservation. If buried on hot coals or ashes, the heat can kill pathogens, the dry ash can desiccate, and the earth can block oxygen and further contamination. If buried where the earth is very cold, the earth acts like a refrigerator.

Controlled Use of Micro-organism

Some foods, such as many cheeses, wines, and beers will keep for a long time because their production uses specific micro-organisms that combat spoilage from other less benign organisms. These micro-organisms keep pathogens in check by creating an environment toxic for themselves and other micro-organisms by producing acid or alcohol. Starter micro-organisms, salt, hops, controlled (usually cool) temperatures, controlled (usually low) levels of oxygen and/or other methods are used to create the specific controlled conditions that will support the desirable organisms that produce food fit for human consumption.

Biopreservation

3D stick model of nisin. Some lactic acid bacteria manufacture nisin. It is a particularly effective preservative.

Biopreservation is the use of natural or controlled microbiota or antimicrobials as a way of preserving food and extending it's shelf life. Beneficial bacteria or the fermentation products produced by these bacteria are used in biopreservation to control spoilage and render pathogens inactive in food. It is a benign ecological approach which is gaining increasing attention.

Of special interest are lactic acid bacteria (LAB). Lactic acid bacteria have antagonistic properties which make them particularly useful as biopreservatives. When LABs compete for nutrients, their metabolites often include active antimicrobials such as lactic and acetic acid, hydrogen peroxide, and peptide bacteriocins. Some LABs produce the antimicrobial nisin which is a particularly effective preservative.

These days LAB bacteriocins are used as an integral part of hurdle technology. Using them in combination with other preservative techniques can effectively control spoilage bacteria and other pathogens, and can inhibiting the activities of a wide spectrum of organisms, including inherently resistant Gram-negative bacteria.

High Pressure Food Preservation

High pressure food preservation refers to high pressure used for food preservation. "Pressed inside a vessel exerting 70,000 pounds per square inch (480 MPa) or more, food can be processed so that it retains its fresh appearance, flavour, texture and nutrients while disabling harmful microorganisms and slowing spoilage." By 2001, adequate commercial equipment was developed so that by 2005 the process was being used for products ranging from orange juice to guacamole to deli meats and widely sold.

Drying Food

Drying is a method of food preservation that works by removing water from the food, which inhibits the growth of microorganisms and hinders quality decay. Drying food using sun and wind to prevent spoilage has been practised since ancient times. Water is usually removed by evaporation (air drying, sun drying, smoking or wind drying) but, in the case of freeze-drying, food is first frozen and then the water is removed by sublimation.

Bacteria yeasts and moulds need the water in the food to grow. Drying effectively prevents them from surviving in the food.

A Whole Potato, Sliced Pieces (Right) and Dried Sliced Pieces (Left)

Many different foods are prepared by dehydration. Good examples are meat such as prosciutto (a.k.a. Parma ham), bresaola, and beef jerky. Dried and salted reindeer meat is a traditional Sami food. First the meat is soaked/pickled in saltwater for a couple of days to guarantee the conservation of the meat. Then the meat is dried in the sun in spring when the air temperature is below zero. The dried meat can be further processed to make soup.

Fruits change character completely when dried: the plum becomes a prune, the grape a raisin; figs and dates are also transformed in new, different products, that can be eaten as they are or else after rehydration.

Home drying of vegetables, fruit and even meat (to produce jerky) may be carried out by a do-it-yourself practice, employing electrical dehydrators (household appliance). If the user does not like to use additives as potassium metabisulphite, or BHA, BHT for meats, dried products may be hermetically shelf stored if it is to be consumed soon, or else in the refrigerator or even freezer if a long storage is to be expected. Freeze dried vegetables are often found in backpackers food, hunters, military, etc. The exception to this rule are bulbs, such as garlic and onion, which are often dried. Also chilis are frequently dried. Edible and psilocybin mushrooms, as well as other fungi, are also sometimes dried for preservation purposes, to affect the potency of chemical components, or so they can be used as seasonings.

For centuries, much of the European diet depended on dried cod, known as salt cod or bacalhau (with salt) or stockfish (without). It formed the main protein source for the slaves on the West Indian plantations, and was a major economic force within the triangular trade. Dried shark meat, known as Hákarl, is a delicacy in Iceland.

Hundreds of millions of tonnes of wheat, corn, soybean, rice and other grains as sorghum, sunflower seeds, rapeseed/canola, barley, oats, etc., are dried in grain dryers. In the main agricultural countries, drying comprises the reduction of moisture from about 17-30 per cent w/w to values between 8 and 15 per cent w/w, depending on the grain. The final moisture content for drying must be adequate for storage.

The more oil the grain has, the lower its storage moisture content will be (though its initial moisture for drying will also be lower). Cereals are often dried to 14 per cent w/w, while oilseeds, to 12.5 per cent (soybeans), 8 per cent (sunflower) and 9 per cent (peanuts). Drying is carried out as a requisite for safe storage, in order to inhibit microbial growth. However, low temperatures in storage are also highly recommended to avoid degradative reactions and, especially, the growth of insects and mites.

A good maximum storage temperature is about 18°C. The largest dryers are normally used 'Off-farm', in elevators, and are of the continuous type: Mixed-flow dryers are preferred in Europe, while Cross-flow dryers in the USA. In Argentina, both types are usually found. Continuous flow dryers may produce up to 100 metric tonnes of dried grain per hour. The depth of grain the air must traverse in continuous dryers range from some 0.15 m in Mixed flow dryers to some 0.30 m in Cross-Flow. Batch dryers are mainly used 'On-Farm', particularly in the USA and Europe.

They normally consist of a bin, with heated air flowing horizontally from an internal cylinder through an inner perforated metal sheet, then through a annular grain bed, some 0.50 m thick (coaxial with the internal cylinder) in radial direction, and finally across the outer perforated metal sheet, before being discharged to the atmosphere.

The usual drying times range from 1 h to 4 h depending on how much water must be removed, type of grain, air temperature and the grain depth. In the USA, continuous counterflow dryers may be found on-farm, adapting a bin to slowly drying grain fed at the top and removed at the bottom of the bin by a sweeping auger. Grain drying is an active area of manufacturing and research. Now it is possible to simulate the performance of a dryer with computer programmes based on equations (mathematical models) that represent the phenomena involved in drying: physics, physical chemistry, thermodynamics and heat and mass transfer.

Most recently the evolution of quality indices is beginning to be predicted with some confidence, in order to add an essential performance parameter with which to establish a compromise of reasonably fast drying rate, limited energy consumption, and satisfactory grain quality. A typical quality parameter in wheat drying is the breadmaking quality and germination percentage whose reductions in drying are somewhat related.

Methods

There are many different methods for drying, each with their own advantages for particular applications; these include:

- Bed dryers
- Drum drying
- Freeze drying
- Shelf dryers
- Spray drying
- Sunlight
- Commercial food dehydrators
- Household oven

3 Frozen Food

Freezing food preserves food from the time it is prepared to the time it is eaten. Since early times, farmers, fishermen, and trappers have preserved their game in unheated buildings during the winter season. Freezing food slows down decomposition by turning water to ice, making it unavailable for most bacterial growth. In the food commodity industry, the process is called IQF or Individually Quick Frozen.

Clarence Birdseye, an American inventor, developed the quick-freezing system. He discovered that the combination of ice, wind, and low temperatures in the Arctic froze anything that was exposed to it almost instantly. Birdseye's soon realized that the quick freezing effectively prevented large ice crystals from forming. Other attempts had resulted in the formation of large crystals, which destroyed the delicate cellular structure of the food. With only an electric fan, a few buckets of brine, and cakes of ice, Clarence Birdseye perfected his system of packing fresh food into waxed cardboard boxes and flash-freezing it under high pressure. He sold the patent to the Goldman-Sachs Trading Corporation (a subsidiary of Goldman Sachs & Company) and the Postum Company. In 1929 the first quick-frozen vegetables were sold to the public.

Preservatives

Frozen foods don't require many preservatives because the process of preparing the food for freezing kills much of the bacteria living on the food. Carboxymethylcellulose (CMC) is used as a stabilizer in frozen foods because of its tasteless and odourless properties.

Packaging

Frozen food packaging must maintain its integrity throughout machine filling, sealing, freezing, storage, transportation, thawing, and often cooking. Most frozen foods are cooked in a microwave oven. To make it easier for the consumer, manufacturers have developed packaging that can go straight from freezer to microwave.

In 1974, the first differential heating container (DHC) was sold to the public. A DHC is a sleeve of metal designed to allow frozen foods to receive the correct amount of heat. Various sized apertures were positioned around the sleeve. The consumer would put the frozen dinner into the sleeve according to what needed the most heat. This ensured proper cooking.

Today there are multiple options for packaging frozen foods. Boxes, cartons, bags, pouches, heat-in-bag pouches, lidded trays and pans, crystallized PET trays, and composite and plastic cans.

Scientists are continually researching new aspects of frozen food packaging. Active packaging offers a host of new technologies that can actively sense and then neutralize the presence of bacteria or other harmful species. Active packaging can extend shelf-life, maintain product safety, and help preserve the food over a longer period of time. Several functions of active packaging are being researched:

- Oxygen scavengers
- Time Temperature Indicators and digital temperature dataloggers
- Antimicrobials

- Carbon Dioxide controllers
- Microwave susceptors
- *Moisture control:* Water activity, Moisture vapour transmission rate, etc.
- Flavour enhancers
- Oder generators
- Oxygen-permeable films
- Oxygen generators
- Validation of cold chain

With these new technologies, food may last longer and our knowledge about its safety will increase.

Vitamin Content of Frozen Foods

Vitamin C: Usually lost in a higher concentration than any other vitamin. A study was performed on peas to determine the cause of Vitamin C loss. A vitamin loss of ten per cent occurred during the blanching phase with the rest of the loss occurring during the cooling and washing stages. The vitamin loss was not actually accredited to the freezing process. Another experiment was performed involving peas and lima beans. Frozen and canned vegetables were both used in the experiment. The frozen vegetable were stored at -10ºF and the canned vegetables were stored at room temperature (75 ºF). After 0, 3, 6, and 12 months of storage, the vegetables were analyzed with and without cooking. O'Hara, the scientist performing the experiment said, "From the view point of the vitamin content of the two vegetables when they were ready for the plate of the consumer, there did not appear to be any marked advantages attributable to method of preservation, frozen storage, processed in a tin, or processed in glass".

Vitamin B_1 (Thiamin): A vitamin loss of 25 per cent is normal. Thiamin is easily soluble in water and is destroyed by heat.

Vitamin B_2 (Riboflavin): Not much research has been done to see how much freezing affects Riboflavin levels. One study found an 18 per cent vitamin loss in green vegetables while another found a 4 per cent loss. It is commonly accepted that the loss of Riboflavin has to do with the preparation for freezing rather than the actual freezing process itself.

Vitamin A (Carotene): There is little loss of Carotene during preparation for freezing and freezing of most vegetables. However, there is a danger of losing the vitamin during a long-continued storage period.

Efficiency

Freezing is an effective form of food preservation because the pathogens that cause food spoilage are killed or do not grow very rapidly at reduced temperatures. The process is less effective in food preservation than are thermal techniques, such as boiling, because pathogens are more likely to be able to survive cold temperatures rather than hot temperatures. One of the problems surrounding the use of freezing as a method of food preservation is the danger that pathogens deactivated (but not killed) by the process will once again become active when the frozen food thaws.

Foods may be preserved for several months by freezing. Long-term frozen storage requires a constant temperature of -18°C (0°F) or less. Some freezers cannot achieve such a low temperature. The time food can be kept in the freezer is reduced considerably if the temperature in a freezer fluctuates; small ice crystals thaw as the temperature moves up, and refreeze onto larger crystals as the temperature declines. Fluctuations can occur by a small gap in the freezer door or adding a large amount of unfrozen food.

Freezing

Freezing or solidification is a phase change in which a liquid turns into a solid when its temperature is lowered below its freezing point. The reverse process is melting.

All known liquids, except liquid helium, freeze when the temperature is lowered enough. Liquid helium remains liquid at atmospheric pressure even at absolute zero, and can be solidified only under pressure. For most substances, the melting and freezing points are the same temperature; however, certain substances possess differing solid-liquid transition temperatures. For example, agar displays a hysteresis in its melting and freezing temperatures. It melts at 85ºC (185ºF) and solidifies from 31ºC to 40ºC (89.6ºF to 104ºF).

Most liquids freeze by crystallization, formation of crystalline solid from the uniform liquid. This is a first-order thermodynamic phase transition, which means that, as long as solid and liquid coexist, the equilibrium temperature of the system remains constant and equal to the melting point. Crystallization consists of two major events, nucleation and crystal growth. Nucleation is the step wherein the molecules start to gather into clusters, on the nanometer scale, arranging in a defined and periodic manner that defines the crystal structure. The crystal growth is the subsequent growth of the nuclei that succeed in achieving the critical cluster size.

Supercooling

In spite of the second law of thermodynamics, crystallization of pure liquids usually begins at lower temperature than the melting point, due to high activation energy of homogeneous nucleation. The creation of a nucleus implies the formation of an interface at the boundaries of the new phase. Some energy is expended to form this interface, based on the surface energy of each phase. If a hypothetical nucleus is too small, the energy that would be released by forming its volume is not enough to create its surface, and nucleation does not proceed. Freezing does not start until the temperature is low enough to provide enough energy to form stable nuclei. In presence of irregularities on the surface of the containing vessel, solid or gaseous impurities, pre-formed solid crystals, or other nucleators, heterogeneous nucleation may occur, where some energy is released by the partial destruction of the previous interface, raising the supercooling point to be near or equal to the melting point. The melting point of water at 1 atmosphere of pressure is very close to 0°C (32°F, 273.15 K), and in the presence of nucleating substances the freezing point of water is close to the melting point, but in the absence of nucleators water can super cool to -40°C (-40°F, 233 K) before freezing. Under high pressure (2,000 atmospheres) water will super cool to as low as -70°C (-94°F, 203 K) before freezing.

Exothermicity

Freezing is an exothermic process, meaning that as liquid changes into solid, heat and pressure is released. This is often seen as counter-intuitive, since the temperature of the material does not rise during freezing, except if the liquid were supercooled. But this can be understood, since heat must be continually removed from the freezing liquid or the freezing process will stop. The energy released upon freezing is a latent heat, and is known as the enthalpy of fusion and is exactly the same as the energy required to melt the same amount of the solid.

Vitrification

Certain materials, such as glass and glycerol, may harden without crystallizing; these are called amorphous solids. Amorphous materials as well as some polymers do not have a true freezing point, as there is no abrupt phase change at any specific temperature. Instead, there is a gradual change in their viscoelastic properties over a range of temperatures. Such materials are characterized by a glass transition that occurs at a glass transition temperature, which may be roughly defined as the 'knee' point of the material's density *vs.* temperature graph.

Freezing of Living Organisms

Many living organisms are able to tolerate prolonged periods of time at temperatures below the freezing point of water. Most living organisms accumulate cryoprotectants such as anti-nucleating proteins, polyols, and glucose to protect themselves against frost damage by sharp ice crystals. Most plants, in particular, can safely reach temperatures of -4°C to

-12°C. Certain bacteria, notably *Pseudomonas syringae*, produce specialized proteins that serve as potent ice nucleators, which they use to force ice formation on the surface of various fruits and plants at about -2°C. The freezing causes injuries in the epithelia and makes the nutrients in the underlying plant tissues available to the bacteria.

Bacteria

Three species of bacteria, *Carnobacterium pleistocenium*, as well as *Chryseobacterium greenlandensis* and *Herminiimonas glaciei*, have reportedly been revived after surviving for thousands of years frozen in ice.

Plants

Many plants undergo a process called hardening, which allows them to survive temperatures below 0°C for weeks to months.

Animals

The nematode *Haemonchus contortus* can survive 44 weeks frozen at liquid nitrogen temperatures. Other nematodes that survive at temperatures below 0°C include *Trichostrongylus colubriformis* and *Panagrolaimus davidi*. Many species of reptiles and amphibians survive freezing. See cryobiology for a full discussion.

Human gametes and 2-, 4- and 8-cell embryos can survive freezing and are viable for up to 10 years, a process known as cryopreservation.

Experimental attempts to freeze human beings for later revival are known as cryonics.

Freezing is a common method of food preservation that slows both food decay and the growth of micro-organisms. Besides the effect of lower temperatures on reaction rates, freezing makes water less available for bacterial growth.

4 Vacuum Packing

Vacuum packing is a method of storing food and presenting it for sale. Appropriate types of food are stored in an airless environment, usually in an air-tight pack or bottle to prevent the growth of microorganisms. The vacuum environment removes atmospheric oxygen, protecting the food from spoiling by limiting the growth of aerobic bacteria or fungi, and preventing the evaporation of volatile components. Vacuum packing is commonly used for long-term storage of dry foods such as cereals, nuts, cured meats, cheese, smoked fish, coffee, and potato chips (crisps). It is also for storage of fresh foods such as vegetables, meats, and liquids such as soups in a shorter term because vacuum condition cannot stop bacteria from getting water which can promote their growth. Vacuum packaging food can extend its life by up to 3-5 times.

Vacuum packing is also used to reduce greatly the bulk of non-food items. For example, clothing and bedding can be stored in bags evacuated with a domestic vacuum cleaner or a dedicated vacuum sealer. This technique is sometimes used to compact household waste, for example where a charge is made for each full bag collected. Vacuum packing can be used to reduce bulk of inflatable items as well.

Vacuum packaging products using plastic bags, canisters, bottles, or mason jars are available for home use.

Vacuum packaging delicate food items can be done by using an inert gas kit, typically available on chamber vacuum sealers. After air has been removed, an inert gas (such as nitrogen) is added to maintain the preservation of packaged food while preventing damage. An example of inert gas for packaging delicate foods is potato chips.

External Sealers

External vacuum sealers involve a bag being attached to the vacuum-sealing machine externally. The machine will remove the air and seal the bag, which is all done outside the machine.

Chamber Sealers

Chamber sealers require the entire product to be placed within the machine. Like external sealers, a plastic bag is typically used for packaging. Once the product is placed in the machine, the lid is closed and air is removed. Once the air is removed, the bag is sealed and the atmosphere within the chamber is returned back to normal. The lid is then opened and the product removed. Chamber sealers are typically used for higher-volume packaging.

Manufacturers of chamber type vacuum packing machines include: Cryovac, Multivac, Sammic, VC999, New Diamond Vac, Jaw Feng Machinery, Sevana and several others.

Preventing Freezer Burn

When foods are frozen without preparation, freezer burn can occur. It happens when the surface of the food is dehydrated, and this leads to a dried and leathery appearance. Freezer burn also ruins the flavour and texture of foods. Vacuum packing prevents freezer burn by preventing the food from exposure to the cold, dry air.

Sous-vide Cooking

Vacuum packaging also allows for a special cooking method, Sous-vide. Sous-vide, meaning 'under vacuum' in French, involves poaching food that is vacuum sealed in a plastic bag.

Security

Due to an oxygen-poor environment, anaerobic microorganism can proliferate, so vacuum packing is often used in combination with other treatment.

Packaging

Packaging is the science, art, and technology of enclosing or protecting products for distribution, storage, sale, and use. Packaging also refers to the *process* of design, evaluation, and production of packages. Packaging can be described as a *coordinated system* of preparing goods for transport, warehousing, logistics, sale, and end use. Packaging contains, protects, preserves, transports, informs, and sells. In many countries it is fully integrated into government, business, institutional, industrial, and personal use.

Package labelling (en-GB) or labelling (en-US) is any written, electronic, or graphic communications on the packaging or on a separate but associated label.

The first packages used the natural materials available at the time: Baskets of reeds, wineskins (Bota bags), wooden boxes, pottery vases, ceramic amphorae, wooden barrels, woven bags, etc. Processed materials were used to form packages as they were developed: for example, early glass and bronze vessels. The study of old packages is an important aspect of archaeology.

The earliest recorded use of paper for packaging dates back to 1035, when a Persian traveller visiting markets in Cairo noted that vegetables, spices and hardware were wrapped in paper for the customers after they were sold.

Iron and tin plated steel were used to make cans in the early 19th century. Paperboard cartons and corrugated fiberboard boxes were first introduced in the late 19th century.

Packaging advancements in the early 20th century included Bakelite closures on bottles, transparent cellophane overwraps and panels on cartons, increased processing efficiency and improved food safety. As additional materials such as aluminum and several types of plastic were developed, they were incorporated into packages to improve performance and functionality.

In-plant recycling has long been common for production of packaging materials. Post-consumer recycling of aluminum and paper based products has been economical for many years: since the 1980s, post-consumer recycling has increased due to curbside recycling, consumer awareness, and regulatory pressure.

As of 2003, the packaging sector accounted for about two percent of the gross national product in developed countries. About half of this market was related to food packaging

Packaging and package labelling have several objectives:

- *Physical protection:* The objects enclosed in the package may require protection from, among other things, mechanical shock, vibration, lectrostatic discharge, compression, temperature, etc.
- *Barrier protection:* A barrier from oxygen, water vapor, dust, etc., is often required. Permeation is a critical factor in design. Some packages contain desiccants or Oxygen absorbers to help extend shelf life. Modified atmospheres or controlled atmospheres are also maintained in some food packages. Keeping the contents clean, fresh, sterile and safe for the intended shelf life is a primary function.
- *Containment or agglomeration:* Small objects are typically grouped together in one package for reasons of efficiency. For example, a single box of 1000 pencils requires less physical handling than 1000 single pencils. Liquids, powders, and granular materials need containment.
- *Information transmission:* Packages and labels communicate how to use, transport, recycle, or dispose of the package or product. With pharmaceuticals, food, medical, and chemical products, some types of information are required by governments. Some packages and labels also are used for track and trace purposes.

- *Marketing:* The packaging and labels can be used by marketers to encourage potential buyers to purchase the product. Package graphic design and physical design have been important and constantly evolving phenomenon for several decades Marketing communications and graphic design are applied to the surface of the package and (in many cases) the point of sale display.
- *Security:* Packaging can play an important role in reducing the security risks of shipment. Packages can be made with improved tamper resistance to deter tampering and also can have tamper-evident features to help indicate tampering. Packages can be engineered to help reduce the risks of package pilferage: Some package constructions are more resistant to pilferage and some have pilfer indicating seals. Packages may include authentication seals and use security printing to help indicate that the package and contents are not counterfeit. Packages also can include anti-theft devices, such as dye-packs, RFID tags, or electronic article surveillance tags that can be activated or detected by devices at exit points and require specialized tools to deactivate. Using packaging in this way is a means of loss prevention.
- *Convenience:* Packages can have features that add convenience in distribution, handling, stacking, display, sale, opening, reclosing, use, dispensing, and reuse.
- *Portion control:* Single serving or single dosage packaging has a precise amount of contents to control usage. Bulk commodities (such as salt) can be divided into packages that are a more suitable size for individual households. It is also aids the control of inventory: selling sealed one-liter-bottles of milk, rather than having people bring their own bottles to fill themselves.

Packaging Types

Packaging may be looked at as being of several different types. For example a transport package or distribution package can be the shipping container used to ship, store, and handle the product or inner packages. Some identify a consumer package as one which is directed toward a consumer or household.

Packaging may be described in relation to the type of product being packaged: medical device packaging, bulk chemical packaging, over-the-counter drug packaging, retail food packaging, military materiel packaging, pharmaceutical packaging, etc.

It is sometimes convenient to categorize packages by layer or function: 'primary', 'secondary', etc.

- *Primary* packaging is the material that first envelops the product and holds it. This usually is the smallest unit of distribution or use and is the package which is in direct contact with the contents.
- *Secondary* packaging is outside the primary packaging, perhaps used to group primary packages together.

Tertiary packaging is used for bulk handling, warehouse storage and transport shipping. The most common form is a palletized unit load that packs tightly into containers.

These broad categories can be somewhat arbitrary. For example, depending on the use, a shrink wrap can be primary packaging when applied directly to the product, secondary packaging when combining smaller packages, and tertiary packaging on some distribution packs.

Symbols Used on Packages and Labels

Many types of symbols for package labelling are nationally and internationally standardized. For consumer packaging, symbols exist for product certifications, trademarks, proof of purchase, etc. Some requirements and symbols exist to communicate aspects of consumer use and safety, for example the estimated sign that notes conformance to EU weights and measures accuracy regulations. Examples of environmental and recycling symbols include the recycling symbol, the resin identification code and the 'Green Dot'.

Bar codes, Universal Product Codes, and RFID labels are common to allow automated information management in logistics and retailing. Country of Origin Labelling is often used.

Shipping Container Labelling

'Print and Apply' corner wrap UCC (GS1-128) label application to a pallet load.

Technologies related to shipping containers are identification codes, bar codes, and electronic data interchange (EDI). These three core technologies serve to enable the business functions in the process of shipping containers throughout the distribution channel. Each has an essential function: identification codes either relate product information or serve as keys to other data, bar codes allow for the automated input of identification codes and other data, and EDI moves data between trading partners within the distribution channel.

Elements of these core technologies include UPC and EAN item identification codes, the SCC-14 (UPC shipping container code), the SSCC-18 (Serial Shipping Container Codes), Interleaved 2-of-5 and UCC/EAN-128 (newly designated GS1-128) bar code symbologies, and ANSI ASC X12 and UN/EDIFACT EDI standards.

Small parcel carriers often have their own formats. For example, United Parcel Service has a MaxiCode 2-D code for parcel tracking.

RFID labels for shipping containers are also increasing in usage. A Wal-Mart division, Sam's Club, has also moved in this direction and is putting pressure on its suppliers for compliance.

Package design and development are often thought of as an integral part of the new product development process. Alternatively, development of a package (or component) can be a separate process, but must be linked closely with the product to be packaged. Package design starts with the identification of all the requirements: structural design, marketing, shelf life, quality assurance, logistics, legal, regulatory, graphic design, end-use, environmental, etc. The design criteria, performance (specified by package testing), completion time targets, resources, and cost constraints need to be established and agreed upon.

An example of how package design is affected by other factors is the relationship to logistics. When the distribution system includes individual shipments by a small parcel carrier, the sortation, handling, and mixed stacking make severe demands on the strength and protective ability of the transport package. If the logistics system consists of uniform palletized unit loads, the structural design of the package can be designed to those specific needs: vertical stacking, perhaps for a longer time frame. A package designed for one mode of shipment may not be suited for another.

With some types of products, the design process involves detailed regulatory requirements for the package. For example with packaging foods, any package components that may contact the food are food contact materials. Toxicologists and food scientists need to verify that the packaging materials are allowed by applicable regulations. Packaging engineers need to verify that the completed package will keep the product safe for its intended shelf life with normal usage. Packaging processes, labelling, distribution, and sale need to be validated to comply with regulations and have the well being of the consumer in mind.

Sometimes the objectives of package development seem contradictory. For example, regulations for an over-the-counter drug might require the package to be tamper-evident and child resistant These intentionally make the package difficult to open. The intended consumer, however, might be handicapped or elderly and be unable to readily open the package. Meeting all goals is a challenge.

Package design may take place within a company or with various degrees of external packaging engineering: independent contractors, consultants, vendor evaluations, independent laboratories, contract packagers, total outsourcing, etc. Some sort of formal Project planning and Project management methodology is required for all but the simplest package design and development programmes. An effective quality management system and Verification and Validation protocols are mandatory for some types of packaging and recommended for all.

Environmental Considerations

Package development involves considerations for sustainability, environmental responsibility, and applicable environmental and recycling regulations. It may involve a life cycle assessment which considers the material and energy inputs and outputs to the package, the packaged product (contents), the packaging process, the logistics system waste management, etc. It is necessary to know the relevant regulatory requirements for point of manufacture, sale, and use.

The traditional 'three R's' of reduce, reuse, and recycle are part of a waste hierarchy which may be considered in product and package development.

The Waste Hierarchy

Prevention: Waste prevention is a primary goal. Packaging should be used only where needed. Proper packaging can also help prevent waste. Packaging plays an important part in preventing loss or damage to the packaged-product (contents). Usually, the energy content and material usage of the product being packaged are much greater than that of the package. A vital function of the package is to protect the product for its intended use: if the product is damaged or degraded, its entire energy and material content may be lost.

Minimization: (also 'source reduction') The mass and volume of packaging (per unit of contents) can be measured and used as one of the criteria to minimize during the package design process. Usually 'reduced' packaging also helps minimize costs. Packaging engineers continue to work toward reduced packaging.

Reuse: The reuse of a package or component for other purposes is encouraged. Returnable packaging has long been useful (and economically viable) for closed loop logistics systems. Inspection, cleaning, repair and recouperage are often needed. Some manufacturers re-use the packaging of the incoming parts for a product, either as packaging for the outgoing product or as part of the product itself.

Recycling: Recycling is the reprocessing of materials (pre- and post-consumer) into new products. Emphasis is focussed on recycling the largest primary components of a package: steel, aluminum, papers, plastics, etc. Small components can be chosen which are not difficult to separate and do not contaminate recycling operations.

Energy recovery: Waste-to-energy and Refuse-derived fuel in approved facilities are able to make use of the heat available from the packaging components.

Disposal: Incineration, and placement in a sanitary landfill are needed for some materials. Certain states within the US regulate packages for toxic contents, which have the potential to contaminate emissions and ash from incineration and leachate from landfill. Packages should not be littered.

Development of sustainable packaging is an area of considerable interest by standards organizations, government, consumers, packagers, and retailers.

A choice of packaging machinery includes: technical capabilities, labor requirements, worker safety, maintainability, serviceability, reliability, ability to integrate into the packaging line, capital cost, floorspace, flexibility (change-over, materials, etc.), energy usage, quality of outgoing packages, qualifications (for food, pharmaceuticals, etc.), throughput, efficiency, productivity, ergonomics, return on investment, etc.

Packaging machinery can be:

- purchased as standard, off-the-shelf;
- purchased custom-made or custom-tailored to specific operations;
- manufactured or modified by in-house engineers and maintenance staff;

Packaging machines may be of the following general types:

- Accumulating and collating machines
- Blister packs, skin packs and vacuum packaging machines
- Bottle caps equipment, over-capping, lidding, closing, seaming and sealing machines
- Box, case and tray forming, packing, unpacking, closing and sealing machines
- Cartoning machines
- Cleaning, sterilizing, cooling and drying machines
- Coding, printing, marking, stamping, and imprinting machines
- Converting machines
- Conveyor belts, accumulating and related machines
- Feeding, orienting, placing and related machines
- Filling machines: handling dry, powered, solid, liquid, gas, or viscous products
- Inspecting, detecting and check weigher machines
- Label dispenser
- Orienting, unscrambling machines
- Package filling and closing machines
- Palletizing, depalletizing, unit load assembly
- Product identification: labelling, marking, etc.
- Wrapping machines: shrink wrap, banding
- Form, fill and seal machines
- Other speciality machinery: slitters, perforating, laser cutters, parts attachment, etc.
- Process machinery (product preparation): Chopper, Crusher, Cutter, Molder, Peeler, etc.
- Process machinery (special product): Coating, Enrobing, Seasoning
- Process machinery (product cooking, heating, and cooling) aseptic.

Curing Food Preservation

Curing refers to various food preservation and flavouring processes, especially of meat or fish, by the addition of a combination of salt, sugar, nitrates or nitrite. Many curing processes also involve smoking.

Food curing dates back to ancient times, both in the form of smoked meat and as salt-cured meat. Although the ancient people curing the meat did not know this, it was actually nitrates present in the salt that helped the curing process. The Native Americans used to hang their meat at the top of their teepees to increase the amount of smoke coming into contact with the food.

CHEMICAL ACTIONS

Salt

Table salt (sodium chloride) is the primary ingredient used in meat curing. Removal of water and addition of salt to meat creates a solute-rich environment where osmotic pressure draws water out of microorganisms, retarding their growth. Doing this requires a concentration of salt of nearly 20 per cent. In addition, salt causes the soluble meat proteins to come to the surface of the meat cut and then solidify, which is what gives sausage its characteristic skin. Finally, salt slows the oxidation process, effectively preventing the meat from going rancid.

Sugar

The sugar added to meat for the purpose of curing it comes in many forms, including honey, corn syrup solids, and maple syrup. However, with the exception of bacon, it does not contribute much to the flavour, but it does alleviate the harsh flavour of the salt. Sugar also contributes to the growth of beneficial bacteria like *Lactobacillus* by feeding them.

Nitrates and nitrites not only help kill bacteria, but also produce a characteristic flavour and give meat a pink or red color. Nitrate (NO_3^-), generally supplied by sodium nitrate or potassium nitrate, is used as a source for nitrite (NO_2^-). The nitrite further breaks down in the meat into nitric oxide (NO), which then binds to the iron atom in the center of myoglobin's heme group, reducing oxidation and causing a reddish-brown colour (nitrosomyoglobin) when raw, and the characteristic cooked-ham pink colour (nitrosohemochrome or nitrosyl-heme) when cooked. The addition of ascorbate to cured meat reduces formation of nitrosamines, but increases the nitrosylation of iron. The use of nitrates in food preservation is controversial, though, due to the potential for the formation of nitrosamines when the preserved food is cooked at high temperature. The usage of either compound is therefore carefully regulated; for example, in the United States, the concentration of nitrates and nitrites is generally limited to 200 ppm or lower. However, they are considered irreplaceable in the prevention of botulinum poisoning from consumption of cured dry sausages by preventing spore germination.

A 2007 study by Columbia University suggests a link between eating cured meats and chronic obstructive pulmonary disease. Nitrites were posited as a possible cause.

Smoke

Meat can also be preserved by smoking, which is to cook the meat in the presence of smoke. (Thus, the meat is usually near a fire.) Slow-cooking meat while smoking it will also keep it tender. One method of smoking calls for a smokehouse with damp wood chips or sawdust.

Smoking (Cooking)

Smoking is the process of flavouring, cooking, or preserving food by exposing it to the smoke from burning or smoldering plant materials, most often wood. Meats and fish are the most common smoked foods, though cheeses, vegetables, and ingredients used to make beverages such as whisky , Rauchbier and *lapsang souchong* tea are also smoked.

In Europe, alder is the traditional smoking wood, but oak is more often used now, and beech to a lesser extent. In North America, hickory, mesquite, oak, pecan, alder, maple, and fruit-tree woods, such as apple, cherry and plum, are commonly used for smoking. Other fuels besides wood can also be employed, sometimes with the addition of flavouring ingredients. Chinese tea-smoking uses a mixture of uncooked rice, sugar, and tea, heated at the base of a wok. Some North American ham and bacon makers smoke their products over burning corncobs. Peat is burned to dry and smoke the barley malt used to make whisky and some beers. In New Zealand, sawdust from the native manuka (tea tree) is commonly used for hot smoking fish. In Iceland, dried sheep dung is used to cold smoke fish, lamb, mutton and whale, resulting in a unique and rather strongly smoked flavour.

Historically, farms in the western world included a small building termed the *smokehouse*, where meats could be smoked and stored. This was generally well-separated from other buildings both because of the fire danger and because of the smoke emanations.

Cold smoking can be used as a flavour enhancer for items such as chicken breasts, beef, pork chops, salmon, scallops, and steak. The item can be cold smoked for just long enough to give some flavour. Some cold smoked foods are baked, grilled, roasted, or sautéed before eating. Smokehouse temperatures for cold smoking are below 100°F (38°C). In this temperature range, foods take on a smoked flavour, but remain relatively moist. Cold smoking does not cook foods.

Hot smoking exposes the foods to smoke and heat in a controlled environment. Although foods that have been hot smoked are often reheated or cooked, they are typically safe to eat without further cooking. Hams and ham hocks are fully cooked once they are properly smoked. Hot smoking occurs within the range of 165°F (74°C) to 185°F (85°C). Within this temperature range, foods are fully cooked, moist, and flavourful. If the smoker is allowed to get hotter than 185°F (85°C), the foods will shrink excessively, buckle, or even split. Smoking at high temperatures also reduces yield, as both moisture and fat are 'cooked' away.

Smoke roasting or smoke baking refers to any process that has the attributes of smoking combined with either roasting or baking. This smoking method is sometimes referred to as 'barbecuing', 'pit baking', or 'pit roasting'. It may be done in a smoke roaster, closed wood-fired masonry oven or barbecue pit, any smoker that can reach above 250°F (121°C), or in a conventional oven by placing a pan filled with hardwood chips on the floor of the oven so the chips smolder and produce a smokebath. However, this should only be done in a well-ventilated area to prevent carbon monoxide poisoning.

Hardwoods are made up mostly of three materials: cellulose, hemicellulose, and lignin. Cellulose and hemicellulose are the basic structural material of the wood cells; lignin acts as a kind of cell-bonding glue. Some softwoods, especially pines and firs, hold significant quantities of resin, which produces a harsh-tasting soot when burned; these woods are not often used for smoking.

Cellulose and hemicellulose are aggregate sugar molecules; when burnt, they effectively caramelize, producing carbonyls, which provide most of the colour components and sweet, flowery, and fruity aromas. Lignin, a highly complex arrangement of interlocked phenolic molecules, also produces a number of distinctive aromatic elements when burnt, including smoky, spicy, and pungent compounds such as guaiacol, phenol, and syringol, and sweeter scents such as the vanilla-scented vanillin and clove-like isoeugenol. Guaiacol is the phenolic compound most responsible for the 'smokey' taste, while syringol is the primary contributor to smokey aroma. Wood also contains small quantities of proteins, which contribute roasted flavours. Many of the odour compounds in wood smoke, especially the phenolic compounds, are unstable, dissipating after a few weeks or months.

A number of wood smoke compounds act as preservatives. Phenol and other phenolic compounds in wood smoke are both antioxidants, which slow rancidification of animal fats, and antimicrobials, which slow bacterial growth. Other antimicrobials in wood smoke include formaldehyde, acetic acid, and other organic acids, which give wood smoke a low pH—about 2.5. Some of these compounds are toxic to people as well, and may have health effects in the quantities found in cooking applications.

Since different species of trees have different ratios of components, various types of wood do impart a different flavour to food. Another important factor is the temperature at which the wood burns. High-temperature fires see the flavour molecules broken down further into unpleasant or flavourless compounds. The optimal conditions for smoke flavour are low, smoldering temperatures between 570 and 750°F (299 and 399°C). This is the temperature of the burning wood itself, not of the smoking environment, which uses much lower temperatures. Woods that are high in lignin content tend to burn hot; to keep them smoldering requires restricted oxygen supplies or a high moisture content. When smoking using wood chips or chunks, the combustion temperature is often raised by soaking the pieces in water before placing them on a fire.

The main characteristics of the offset smoker are that the cooking chamber is usually cylindrical in shape, with a shorter, smaller diameter cylinder attached to the bottom of one end for a firebox. To cook the meat, a small fire is lit in the firebox, where airflow is tightly controlled. The heat and smoke from the fire is drawn through a connecting pipe or opening into the cooking chamber. The heat and smoke cook and flavour the meat before escaping through an exhaust vent at the opposite end of the cooking chamber. Most manufacturers' models are based on this simple but effective design, and this is what most people picture when they think of a 'BBQ smoker'. Even large capacity commercial units use this same basic design of a separate, smaller fire box and a larger cooking chamber.

The UDS

The Upright Drum Smoker (also referred to as an Ugly Drum Smoker or UDS) is exactly what its name suggests; an upright steel drum that has been modified for the purpose of pseudo-indirect hot smoking. There are many ways to accomplish this, but the basics include the use of a complete steel drum, a basket to hold charcoal near the bottom, and cooking rack (or racks) near the top; all covered by a vented lid of some sort. They have been built using many different sizes of steel drums (30 gallon, 55 gallon, and 85 gallon for example), but the most popular size is the common 55 gallon drum.

This design is similar to smoking with indirect heat due to the distance from the coals and the racks (typically 24"). The temperatures used for smoking are controlled by limiting the amount of air intake at the bottom of the drum, and allowing a similar amount of exhaust out of vents in the lid. UDSs are very efficient with fuel consumption and flexible in their abilities to produce proper smoking conditions, with or without the use of a water pan or drip pan. Most UDS builders/ users would say a water pan defeats the true pit BBQ nature of the UDS, as the drippings from the smoked meat should land on the coals, burning up, and imparting a unique flavour one cannot get with a water pan.

Vertical Water Smoker

A vertical water smoker (also referred to as a bullet smoker because of its shape) is a variation of the upright drum smoker. It uses charcoal or wood to generate smoke and heat, and contains a water bowl between the fire and the cooking grates. The water bowl serves to hold the temperature down and also to add humidity to the smoke chamber. In addition, the bowl catches any drippings from the meat that may cause a flare up. Vertical water smokers are extremely temperature stable and require very little adjustment once the desired temperature has been reached. Because of their relatively low cost and stable temperature, they are sometimes used in barbecue competitions where propane and electric smokers are not allowed.

A propane smoker is designed to allow the smoking of meat in a somewhat more controlled environment. The primary differences are the sources of heat and of the smoke. In a propane smoker, the heat is generated by a gas burner directly under a steel or iron box containing the wood or charcoal that provides the smoke. The steel box has few vent holes, on the top of the box only. By starving the heated wood of oxygen, it smokes instead of burning. Any combination of woods and charcoal may used. This method uses less wood.

Smoke Box Method

This more traditional method uses a two box system: The fire box and the food box. The fire box is typically adjacent or under the cooking box, and can be controlled to a finer degree. The heat and smoke from the fire box exhausts into the food box, where it is used to cook and smoke the meat. These may be as simple as an electric heating element with a pan of wood chips placed on it, although more advanced models have finer temperature controls.

Commercial Smoke House

Commercial smokehouses, mostly made from stainless steel, have independent systems for smoke generation and cooking. Smoke generators use friction, an electric coil or a small flame to ignite sawdust on demand. Heat from steam coils or gas flames is balanced with live steam or water sprays to control the temperature and humidity. Elaborate air handling systems reduce hot or cold spots, to reduce variation in the finished product. Racks on wheels or rails are used to hold the product and facilitate movement.

Smoke is an antimicrobial and antioxidant, but smoke alone is insufficient for preserving food in practice, unless combined with another preservation method. The main problem is the smoke compounds adhere only to the outer surfaces of the food; smoke does not actually penetrate far into meat or fish. In modern times, almost all smoking is carried out for its flavour. Artificial smoke flavouring can be purchased as a liquid to mimic the flavour of smoking, but not its preservative qualities.

In the past, smoking was a useful preservation tool, in combination with other techniques, most commonly salt-curing or drying. In some cases, particularly in climates without much hot sunshine, smoking was simply an unavoidable side effect of drying over a fire. For some long-smoked foods, the smoking time also served to dry the food. Drying, curing, or other techniques can render the interior of foods inhospitable to bacterial life, while the smoking gives the vulnerable exterior surfaces an extra layer of protection. For oily fish smoking is especially useful, as its antioxidant properties delay surface fat rancidification. (Interior fat is not as exposed to oxygen, which is what causes rancidity.) Some heavily-salted, long-smoked fish can keep without refrigeration for weeks or months. Such heavily-preserved foods usually require a treatment such as boiling in fresh water to make them palatable before eating.

6 Sugaring

Sugaring is a food preservation method similar to pickling. Sugaring is the process of desiccating a food by first dehydrating it, then packing it with pure sugar. This sugar can be crystalline in the form of table or raw sugar, or it can be a high sugar density liquid such as honey, syrup or molasses.

The purpose of sugaring is to create an environment hostile to microbial life and prevent food spoilage. Sugaring is commonly used to preserve fruits as well as vegetables such as ginger. From time to time sugaring has also been used for non-food preservations. For example, honey was used as part of the mummification process in some ancient Egyptian rites.

A risk in sugaring is that sugar itself attracts moisture. Once a sufficient moisture level is reached, native yeast in the environment will come out of dormancy and begin to ferment the sugars into alcohol and carbon dioxide. This leads to the process of fermentation. Although fermentation can be used as a food preservation method, it must be intentionally controlled, or the results will tend to be unpleasant.

Pickling

Pickling, also known as brining or corning is the process of preserving food by anaerobic fermentation in brine (a solution of salt in water) to produce lactic acid, or marinating and storing it in an acid solution, usually vinegar (acetic acid). The resulting food is called a *pickle*. This procedure gives the food a salty or sour taste. In South Asia, edible oils are used as the pickling medium with vinegar.

Another distinguishing characteristic is a pH less than 4.6 which is sufficient to kill most bacteria. Pickling can preserve perishable foods for months. Antimicrobial herbs and spices, such as mustard seed, garlic, cinnamon or cloves, are often added. If the food contains sufficient moisture, a pickling brine may be produced simply by adding dry salt. For example, sauerkraut and Korean kimchi are produced by salting the vegetables to draw out excess water. Natural fermentation at room temperature, by lactic acid bacteria, produces the required acidity. Other pickles are made by placing vegetables in vinegar. Unlike the canning process, pickling (which includes fermentation) does not require that the food be completely sterile before it is sealed. The acidity or salinity of the solution, the temperature of fermentation, and the exclusion of oxygen determine which microorganisms dominate, and determine the flavour of the end product.

When both salt concentration and temperature are low, *Leuconostoc mesenteroides* dominates, producing a mix of acids, alcohol, and aroma compounds. At higher temperatures *Lactobacillus plantarum* dominates, which produces primarily lactic acid. Many pickles start with *Leuconostoc*, and change to *Lactobacillus* with higher acidity.

Pickling began as a way to preserve food for out-of-season use and for long journeys, especially by sea. Salt pork and salt beef were common staples for sailors before the days of steam engines.

Although the process was invented to preserve foods, pickles are also made and eaten because people enjoy the resulting flavours. Pickling may also improve the nutritional value of food by introducing B vitamins produced by bacteria.

Pickle Etymology

The term *pickle* is derived from the Dutch word *pekel*, meaning *brine*. In the U.S. and Canada, the word *pickle* alone almost always refers to a pickled cucumber (other types of pickles will be described as 'pickled onion', 'pickled cauliflower', etc.), except when it is used figuratively.

POPULARITY OF PICKLES AROUND THE WORLD

Asia

India has a large variety of pickles (known as *Achar* in Punjabi and Hindi, *Uppinakaayi* in Kannada, *Lonacha* in Marathi, *Oorukai* in Tamil, *ooragaya* in Telugu, which are mainly made from Mango, Lime, Indian Goose Berry (Anwla), Chilli, vegetables, Ginger, Garlic and Citron. These fruits/vegetables are generally mixed with some other ingredients *i.e.* salt, spices, vegetable oils and is set to mature.

In Pakistan, pickles are known locally as *Achaar* (in Urdu) and come in a variety of flavours. Amongst some of the most popular is the traditional mixed Hyderabadi pickle, a common delicacy and staple prepared out of an assortment of fruits (most notably mangos) and vegetables blended with selected spices.

Indonesian pickles, *acar,* are typically made out of cucumber, carrot, bird's eye chilies, and shallots, these items being seasoned with vinegar, sugar and salt. Fruits, such as papaya and pineapple are also sometimes pickled. In the Philippines, *achara* is primarily made out of green papaya, carrots, and shallots, with cloves of garlic and vinegar. In Vietnam, vegetable pickles are called *c?i chua* ('sour vegetables'). In Sri Lanka, *achcharu* is traditionally prepared out of carrots, onions, and ground dates. Mixed with mustard powder, ground pepper, crushed ginger, garlic and vinegar, these items are seasoned in a clay pot.

China is home to a huge variety of pickled vegetables, including radish, *baicai* (Chinese cabbage, notably *suan cai, la bai cai, pao cai,* and Tianjin preserved vegetable), *zha cai,* chili pepper and cucumber, among many others.

Japanese *tsukemono* (pickled foods) include *takuan* (daikon), *umeboshi* (ume plum), *gari* and *beni shoga* (ginger), turnip, cucumber, and Chinese cabbage.

The Korean staple kimchi is usually made from pickled Chinese cabbage and radish, but is also made from green onions, garlic stems, chives and a host of other vegetables. Jangajji is another example of pickled vegetables.

Europe

In Greece, pickles are made out of carrots, celery, eggplants stuffed with diced carrots, cauliflower, tomatoes, and peppers.

In Albania, Bulgaria, Serbia, and Macedonia, mixed pickles, known as *turshi,* form popular appetizers, which are typically eaten with *Rakia*. Pickled green tomatoes, cucumbers, carrots, bell peppers, peppers, eggplants, and sauerkraut are also popular.

In Poland, the traditional pickles are cucumbers and cabbage, but other pickled fruits and vegetables, including plums, pumpkins and mushrooms are also common.

In Romania, pickles are made out of beetroot, cucumbers, green tomatoes (*gogonele*), carrots, cabbage, bell peppers, melons, mushrooms, turnips, celery and cauliflower. Meat, like pork can also be preserved in salt and lard.

In Russia, pickled items include beets, mushrooms, tomatoes, cabbage, cucumbers, ramsons, garlic, eggplant (which is typically stuffed with julienned carrots), custard squash, and watermelon.

Pickled herring, rollmops, and salmon are popular in Scandinavia.

In Turkey, pickles, called *tursu*, are made out of vegetables, roots, and fruits such as peppers, cucumber, Armenian cucumber, cabbage, tomato, eggplant (aubergine), carrot, turnip, beetroot, green almond, baby watermelon, baby cantelope, and green plum. A mixture of spices flavour the pickles.

In Britain, pickled onions and pickled eggs are often sold in pubs and fish and chip shops. Pickled beetroot, walnuts, and gherkins, and condiments such as Branston Pickle and piccalilli are typically eaten as an accompaniment to pork pies and cold meats, sandwiches or a ploughman's lunch. Other popular pickles in the UK are pickled mussels, cockles, red cabbage, mango chutney, sauerkraut, and olives.

In Ukraine, garden produce is commonly pickled using salt, dill, currant leaves and garlic and is stored in a cool, dark place.

In Italy, pickled vegetables, giardiniera, include onions, carrots, celery and cauliflower.

Middle East

In Iran, Israel and all Arab countries, pickles (called *torshi* in Persian, *mekhallel* in Arabic, and *hamutzim* in Hebrew) are commonly made from turnips, peppers, carrots, green olives, cucumbers, beetroot, cabbage, lemons, and cauliflower.

North America

In the United States and Canada, pickled cucumbers (most often referred to simply as "pickles" in Canada and the United States), olives, and sauerkraut are most popular, although pickles popular in other nations (such as the pickled tomatoes commonly offered in New York City delicatessens) are also available. Giardiniera, a mixture of pickled peppers, celery and olives, is a popular condiment in Chicago and other cities with large Italian-American populations, and is often consumed with Italian beef sandwiches. Pickled eggs are common in the Upper Peninsula of Michigan. In the Southern United States, pickled okra and watermelon rind are popular, as are deep-fried pickles and pickled pig's feet,lips chicken eggs and quail eggs.

In Mexico, chile peppers, particularly of the Jalapeño and serrano varieties, pickled with onions, carrots and herbs form common condiments.

The Pickling Process

In chemical pickling, the jar and lid are first boiled in order to sterilize them. The fruits or vegetables to be pickled are then added to the jar along with brine and/or vinegar as well as spices and are then allowed to ferment until the desired taste is obtained. In commercial pickling, a preservative like sodium benzoate or EDTA may also be added to enhance shelf life. In fermentation pickling, the food itself produces the preservation agent, typically by a process that produces lactic acid.

Fermentation (Food)

Fermentation in food processing typically is the conversion of carbohydrates to alcohols and carbon dioxide or organic acids using yeasts, bacteria, or a combination thereof, under anaerobic conditions. A more restricted definition of fermentation is the chemical conversion of sugars into ethanol. The science of fermentation is known as zymurgy.

Fermentation usually implies that the action of microorganisms is desirable, and the process is used to produce alcoholic beverages such as wine, beer, and cider. Fermentation is also employed in the leavening of bread, and for preservation techniques to create lactic acid in sour foods such as sauerkraut, dry sausages, kimchi and yogurt, or vinegar (acetic acid) for use in pickling foods. Natural fermentation precedes human history. Since ancient times, however, humans have been controlling the fermentation process. The earliest evidence of winemaking dates from eight thousand years ago, in Georgia, in the Caucasus area. Seven-thousand-year-old jars containing the remains of wine have been excavated in the Zagros Mountains in Iran, which are now on display at the University of Pennsylvania. There is strong evidence that people were fermenting beverages in Babylon circa 5000 BC, ancient Egypt circa 3150 BC, pre-Hispanic Mexico circa 2000 BC, and Sudan circa 1500 BC. There is also evidence of leavened bread in ancient Egypt circa 1500 BC and of milk fermentation in Babylon circa 3000 BC.

French chemist Louis Pasteur was the first known *zymologist*, when in 1854 he connected yeast to fermentation. Pasteur originally defined fermentation as "respiration without air". Pasteur performed careful research and concluded.

"I am of the opinion that alcoholic fermentation never occurs without simultaneous organization, development and multiplication of cells…If asked, in what consists the chemical act whereby the sugar is decomposed…I am completely ignorant of it."

Contributions to Biochemistry

When studying the fermentation of sugar to alcohol by yeast, Louis Pasteur concluded that the fermentation was catalyzed by a vital force, called 'ferments', within the yeast cells. The 'ferments' were thought to function only within living organisms. "Alcoholic fermentation is an act correlated with the life and organization of the yeast cells, not with the death or putrefaction of the cells", he wrote.

Nevertheless, it was known that yeast extracts ferment sugar even in the absence of living yeast cells. While studying this process in 1897, Eduard Buchner of Humboldt University of Berlin, Germany, found that sugar was fermented even when there were no living yeast cells in the mixture, by a yeast secretion that he termed *zymase*. In 1907 he received the Nobel Prize in Chemistry for his research and discovery of "cell-free fermentation."

The primary benefit of fermentation is the conversion of sugars and other carbohydrates, e.g., converting juice into wine, grains into beer, carbohydrates into carbon dioxide to leaven bread, and sugars in vegetables into preservative organic acids.

Food fermentation has been said to serve five main purposes:

- ❖ Enrichment of the diet through development of a diversity of flavours, aromas, and textures in food substrates.
- ❖ Preservation of substantial amounts of food through lactic acid, alcohol, acetic acid and alkaline fermentations.
- ❖ Biological enrichment of food substrates with protein, essential amino acids, essential fatty acids, and vitamins.

- Elimination of antinutrients.
- A decrease in cooking times and fuel requirements.

Some fermentation products (*e.g.*, fusel alcohol) are deleterious.

Fermented Foods by Region

Worldwide: alcohol, wine, vinegar, olives, yogurt, bread, cheese.

East and Southeast Asia: amazake, asinan, atsara, baiming, belacan, burong mangga, com ruou, dalok, doenjang douchi, jeruk, ambanog, kimchi kombucha, leppet-so, narezushi miang, miso, ata de coco, nata de pina, natto, naw-mai-dong, oncom, pak-siam-dong, paw-tsaynob prahok, ruou nep, sake, seokbakji, soy sauce, stinky tofu, szechwan cabbage tai-tan tsoi, chiraki, tape, tempeh, totkal kimchi, yen tsai zha cai.

Central Asia: kumis (mare milk), kefir, shubat (camel milk).

India: achar, appam, dosa, dhokla, dahi yogurt), idli, mixed pickle, u-to-nga (Northeast fermented fish).

Nepal: achar, dahi (yogurt), gundruk, *jaand* (rice beer), sinki, tongba, Panir.

Africa: fermented millet porridge, garri, hibiscus seed, hot pepper sauce, injera, lamoun makbouss, laxoox, mauoloh, msir, mslalla, oilseed, ogi, ogili, ogiri.

Americas: chicha, elderberry wine, kombucha, pickling (pickled vegetables), sauerkraut, lupin seed, oilseed, chocolate, vanilla, tabasco, tibicos.

Middle East: kushuk, lamoun makbouss, mekhalel, torshi, boza.

Europe: rakfisk, sauerkraut, ogórek kiszony, surströmming, mead, elderberry wine, salami, prosciutto, cultured milk products such as quark kefir, filmjölk, crème fraîche, smetana, skyr.

Oceania: poi, kaanga pirau (rotten corn), sago foods.

Alaska has witnessed a steady increase of cases of botulism since 1985. Despite its small population, it has more cases of botulism than any other state in the United States of

America. This is caused by the traditional Eskimo practice of allowing animal products such as whole fish, fish heads, walrus, sea lion and whale flippers, beaver tails, seal oil, birds, etc., to ferment for an extended period of time before being consumed. The risk is exacerbated when a plastic container is used for this purpose instead of the old-fashioned method, a grass-lined hole, as the botulinum bacteria thrive in the anaerobic conditions created by the air-tight enclosure in plastic.

7 Food Processing

Food processing is the set of methods and techniques used to transform raw ingredients into food or to transform food into other forms for consumption by humans or animals either in the home or by the food processing industry. Food processing typically takes clean, harvested crops or butchered animal products and uses these to produce attractive, marketable and often long shelf-life food products. Similar processes are used to produce animal feed.

Extreme examples of food processing include the delicate preparation of deadly fugu fish or preparing space food for consumption under zero gravity.

Food processing dates back to the prehistoric ages when crude processing incorporated slaughtering, fermenting, sun drying, preserving with salt, and various types of cooking (such as roasting, smoking, steaming, and oven baking). Salt-preservation was especially common for foods that constituted warrior and sailors' diets, up until the introduction of canning methods. This holds true except for lettuce.

Evidence for the existence of these methods can be found in the writings of the ancient Greek , Chaldean, Egyptian and Roman civilizations as well as archaeological evidence from Europe, North and South America and Asia.

These tried and tested processing techniques remained essentially the same until the advent of the industrial revolution. Examples of ready-meals also exist from pre-industrial revolution times such as the Cornish pasty and Haggis. During ancient times and today these are considered processing foods.

Modern food processing technology in the 19th and 20th century was largely developed to serve military needs. In 1809 Nicolas Appert invented a vacuum bottling technique that would supply food for French troops, and this contributed to the development of tinning and then canning by Peter Durand in 1810.

Although initially expensive and somewhat hazardous due to the lead used in cans, canned goods would later become a staple around the world. Pasteurization, discovered by Louis Pasteur in 1862, was a significant advance in ensuring the micro-biological safety of food.

In the 20th century, World War II, the space race and the rising consumer society in developed countries (including the United States) contributed to the growth of food processing with such advances as spray drying, juice concentrates, freeze drying and the introduction of artificial sweeteners, colouring agents, and preservatives such as sodium benzoate.

In the late 20th century products such as dried instant soups, reconstituted fruits and juices, and self cooking meals such as MRE food ration were developed.

In western Europe and North America, the second half of the 20th century witnessed a rise in the pursuit of convenience. Food processing companies marketed their products especially towards middle-class working wives and mothers. Frozen foods (often credited to Clarence Birdseye) found their success in sales of juice concentrates and 'TV dinners'. Processors utilised the perceived value of time to appeal to the postwar population, and this same appeal contributes to the success of convenience foods today.

Benefits

Benefits of food processing include toxin removal, preservation, easing marketing and distribution tasks, and increasing food consistency. In addition, it increases seasonal availability of many foods, enables transportation of delicate perishable foods across long distances and makes many kinds of foods safe to eat by de-activating spoilage and pathogenic micro-organisms. Modern supermarkets would not be feasible without modern food processing techniques, long voyages would not be possible and military campaigns would be significantly more difficult and costly to execute.

Processed foods are usually less susceptible to early spoilage than fresh foods and are better suited for long distance transportation from the source to the consumer. When they were first introduced, some processed foods helped to alleviate food shortages and improved the overall nutrition of populations as it made many new foods available to the masses.

Processing can also reduce the incidence of food borne disease. Fresh materials, such as fresh produce and raw meats, are more likely to harbour pathogenic micro-organisms (*e.g.* Salmonella) capable of causing serious illnesses.

The extremely varied modern diet is only truly possible on a wide scale because of food processing. Transportation of more exotic foods, as well as the elimination of much hard labour gives the modern eater easy access to a wide variety of food unimaginable to their ancestors.

The act of processing can often improve the taste of food significantly.

Mass production of food is much cheaper overall than individual production of meals from raw ingredients. Therefore, a large profit potential exists for the manufacturers and suppliers of processed food products. Individuals may see a benefit in convenience, but rarely see any direct financial cost benefit in using processed food as compared to home preparation.

Processed food freed people from the large amount of time involved in preparing and cooking 'natural' unprocessed foods. The increase in free time allows people much more choice in life style than previously allowed. In many families the adults are working away from home and therefore there is little time for the preparation of food based on fresh ingredients.

The food industry offers products that fulfill many different needs: From peeled potatoes that only have to be boiled at home to fully prepared ready meals that can be heated up in the microwave oven within a few minutes.

Modern food processing also improves the quality of life for people with allergies, diabetics, and other people who cannot consume some common food elements. Food processing can also add extra nutrients such as vitamins.

Drawbacks

In general, fresh food that has not been processed other than by washing and simple kitchen preparation, may be expected to contain a higher proportion of naturally-occurring vitamins, fiber and minerals than an equivalent product processed by the food industry. Vitamin C, for example, is destroyed by heat and therefore canned fruits have a lower content of vitamin C than fresh ones. Often nutrients are deliberately removed from food in an effort to improve its longevity, appearance, or taste.

This process is widespread in examples such as bread, pasta, and pre-made meals. As a result, processed foods often have a higher ratio of calories to other essential nutrients than unprocessed foods, a phenomenon referred to as 'empty calories'.

Food processing can introduce hazards not encountered with naturally-occurring products. Processed foods often include food additives, such as flavourings and texture-enhancing agents, which may have little or no nutritive value, or be unhealthy. Preservatives added or created during processing to extend the 'shelf-life' of commercially-available products, such as nitrites or sulphites, may cause adverse health effects.

In the European Union, only food additives (*e.g.*, sweeteners, preservatives, stabilisers) that have been approved as safe for human consumption by the European Food Safety Authority (EFSA) are allowed, at specified levels, for use in food products. Approved additives receive an E number (E for Europe), which at the same time simplifies communication about food additives in the list of ingredients across the different languages of the EU.Use of low-cost ingredients that mimic the properties of natural ingredients (*e.g.* cheap chemically-hardened vegetable oils in place of more-expensive natural saturated fats or cold-pressed oils) have been shown to cause severe health problems, but are still in widespread use because of cost concerns and lack of consumer knowledge about the effects of substitute ingredients.

Sugars and salts are usually added to processed foods as preservatives and to improve the flavour of the food. As a result eating large amounts of processed foods can lead to excessive intake of these substances, which can then lead to a variety of health complications including high blood pressure, weight gain, and diabetes.

Ingredients in processed foods are often of low quality but are 'disguised' by use of processing.

Because processed food ingredients are often produced in high quantities and distributed widely amongst value-added food manufacturers, failures in hygiene standards in 'low-level' manufacturing facilities that produce a widely-distributed basic ingredient can have serious consequences for many final products.

The addition of these many chemicals for preservation and flavour have been known to cause human and animal cells to grow rapidly, without going into Apoptosis.

The environmental and social pracitices of food processors are often of a low quality. Because of cost pressures and the ability to disguise ingredients in the product, processors are often unconcerned by environmental or social standards. Animals killed for food processing are often kept in industrial farms with low animal welfare standards.

Some commentators, Michael Pollan for example, believe that the excessive consumption of food processing has had a number of negative cultural consequences. For example, people eat more quickly, and less socially than they used to. Food has become too practical and less something to be enjoyed. People are not as aware of the way food is grown and the natural cycle of the planet.

Performance Parameters for Food Processing

When designing processes for the food industry the following performance parameters may be taken into account:

- Hygiene, *e.g.* measured by number of micro-organisms per ml of finished product;
- Energy efficiency measured *e.g.* by "ton of steam per ton of sugar produced";
- Minimization of waste, measured *e.g.* by "percentage of peeling loss during the peeling of potatoes';
- Labour used, measured *e.g.* by "number of working hours per ton of finished product";
- Minimization of cleaning stops measured *e.g.* by "number of hours between cleaning stops".

Cost Reduction

Profit Incentive drives most of the factors behind any industry; the food industry not least of all. Health concerns are generally subservient to profit potential, leading the food processing industry to often ignore major health concerns raised by the use of industrially-produced ingredients (partially-hydrogenated vegetable oils, for example, a well-known and well-researched cause of heart disease, that is still commonly used in processed food to increase profit margin.) Consumer pressure has led to a reduction in the use of industrially-produced ingredients in processed food, but the (often slight) potential for increased profits has barred widespread acceptance by the industry of recognized health problems caused by over-consumption of processed foods.

Often farmers take most of the burden in cost reduction because they're usually submitted to a monopsony by food processing industries.

Health

Reduction of fat content in final product *e.g.* by using baking instead of deep-frying in the production of potato chips, another processed food.

Maintaining the natural taste of the product *e.g.* by using less artificial sweetener than they used before.

Hygiene

The rigorous application of industry and government endorsed standards to minimise possible risk and hazards. The international standard adopted is HACCP.

Efficiency

Rising energy costs lead to increasing usage of energy-saving technologies, *e.g.* frequency converters on electrical drives, heat insulation of factory buildings and heated vessels, energy recovery systems, keeping a single fish frozen all the way from China to Switzerland.

Factory automation systems (often Distributed control systems) reduce personnel costs and may lead to more stable production results.

Industries

Food processing industries and practices include the following:

- ❖ Cannery
- ❖ Fish processing
- ❖ Industrial rendering
- ❖ Meat packing plant

- ❖ Slaughterhouse
- ❖ Sugar industry
- ❖ Vegetable packing plant

Food Industry

The food industry is a complex, global collective of diverse businesses that together supply much of the food energy consumed by the world population. Only subsistence farmers, those who survive on what they grow, can be considered outside of the scope of the modern food industry.

The food industry includes:

- ❖ *Regulation:* local, regional, national and international rules and regulations for food production and sale, including food quality and ood safety, and industry lobbying activities.
- ❖ *Education:* academic, vocational, consultancy.
- ❖ *Research and development:* food technology.
- ❖ *Financial services:* insurance, credit.
- ❖ *Manufacturing:* agri-chemicals, seed, farm machinery and supplies, agricultural construction, etc.
- ❖ *Agriculture:* raising of crops and livestock, seafood.
- ❖ *Food processing:* preparation of fresh products for market, manufacture of prepared food products.
- ❖ *Marketing:* promotion of generic products (*e.g.* milk board), new products, public opinion through advertising, packaging, public relations, etc.
- ❖ *Wholesale and distribution:* warehousing, transportation, logistics.

Definitions

It is challenging to find an inclusive way to cover all aspects of food production and sale. The Food Standards Agency, a government body in the UK, describes it thus:

> "...the whole food industry — from farming and food production, packaging and distribution, to retail and catering".

The Economic Research Service of the USDA uses the term *food system* to describe the same thing:

> "The U.S. food system is a complex network of farmers and the industries that link to them. Those links include makers of farm equipment and chemicals as well as firms that provide services to agri-businesses, such as providers of transportation and financial services. The system also includes the food marketing industries that link farms to consumers, and which include food and fiber processors, wholesalers, retailers, and foodservice establishments".

Industry Size

Processed food sales worldwide are approximately US$3.2 trillion (2004).

In the U.S., consumers spend approximately US$1 trillion annually on food, or nearly 10 per cent of the Gross Domestic Product (GDP). Over 16.5 million people are employed in the food industry.

Agriculture

Agriculture is the process of producing food, feed, fiber and other desired products by the cultivation of certain plants and the raising of domesticated animals (livestock). The practice of agriculture is also known as 'farming', while scientists, inventors and others devoted to improving farming methods and implements are also said to be engaged in agriculture. More people in the world are involved in agriculture as their primary economic activity than in any other, yet it only accounts for four per cent of the world's Gross Domestic Product (GDP).

Food Processing

Food processing is the methods and techniques used to transform raw ingredients into food for human consumption. Food processing takes clean, harvested or slaughtered and butchered components and uses them to produce marketable food products. There are several ways in which food can be produced.

One off production: This method is used when customers make an order for something to be made to their own specifications, for example a wedding cake. The making of One Off Products could take days depending on how intricate the design is and also the ability of the chef making the product.

Batch production: This method is used when the size of the market for a product is not clear, and where there is a range within a product line. A certain number of the same goods will be produced to make up a batch or run, for example at Gregg's Bakery they will bake a certain number of chicken bakes. This method involves estimating the amount of customers that will want to buy that product.

Mass production: This method is used when there is a mass market for a large number of identical products, for example, chocolate bars, ready meals and canned food. The product passes from one stage of production to another along a production line.

Just in time: This method of production is mainly used in sandwich bars such as Subway. All the components of the product are there and the customer chooses what they want in their product and it is made for them fresh in front of them.

Wholesale and Distribution

A vast global transportation network is required by the food industry in order to connect its numerous parts. These include suppliers, manufacturers, warehousing, retailers and the end consumers. There are also companies that add vitamins, minerals, and other necessary requirements during processing to make up for those lost during preparation.

Wholesale markets for fresh food products have tended to decline in importance in OECD countries as well as in Latin America and some Asian countries as a result of the growth of supermarkets, which procure directly from farmers or through preferred suppliers, rather than going through markets.

The constant and uninterrupted flow of product from distribution centers to store locations is a critical link in food industry operations. Distribution centres run more efficiently, throughput can be increased, costs can be lowered, and manpower better utilized if the proper steps are taken when setting up a material handling system in a warehouse.

Retail

With populations around the world concentrating in urban areas, food buying is increasingly removed from all aspects of food production. This is a relatively recent development, having taken place mainly over the last 50 years.

The supermarket is the defining retail element of the food industry, where tens of thousands of products are gathered in one location, in continuous, year-round supply. Restaurants, Cafes, Bakeries and Mobile trucks are also ways consumers can purchase food.

Food preparation is another area where change in recent decades has been dramatic. Today, two food industry sectors are in apparent competition for the retail food dollar. The grocery industry sells fresh and largely raw products for consumers to use as ingredients in home cooking. The food service industry by contrast offers prepared food, either as finished products, or as partially prepared components for final 'assembly'.

Food Industry Technologies

Sophisticated technologies define modern food production. They include many areas. Agricultural machinery, originally led by the tractor, has practically eliminated human labour in many areas of production. Biotechnology is driving much change, in areas as diverse as agrochemicals, plant breeding and food processing. Many other areas of technology are also involved, to the point where it is hard to find an area that does not have a direct impact on the food industry.

Computer technology is also a central force, with computer networks and specialized software providing the support infrastructure to allow global movement of the myriad components involved.

Marketing

As consumers grow increasingly removed from food production, the role of product creation, advertising, publicity become the primary vehicles for information about food. With processed food as the dominant category, marketers have almost infinite possibilities in product creation.

Media and Marketing

A key tool for FMCG marketing managers targeting the supermarket industry includes national titles like *The Grocer* in the U.K., *Checkout* in Ireland, *Progressive Grocer* in the U.S., and *Private Label Europe* for the entire of the European Union.

Labour and Education

Until the last 100 years, agriculture was labour intensive. Farming was a common occupation. Food production flowed from millions of farms. Farmers, largely trained from generation to generation, carried on the family business. That situation has changed dramatically. In North America, over 50 per cent of the population were farm families only a few decades ago; now, that figure is around 1-2 per cent, and about 80 per cent of the population lives in cities. The food industry as a complex whole requires an incredibly wide range of skills. Several hundred occupation types exist within the food industry.

Research and Development

Research in agricultural and food processing technologies happens in great part in university research environments. Projects are often funded by companies from the food industry. There is therefore a direct relationship between the academic and commercial sectors, as far as scientific research.

Prominent Food Companies

- Nestlé is the world's largest food and beverage company.

- Pepsico is the largest U.S. based food and beverage company.
- Unilever is an Anglo-Dutch company that owns many of the world's consumer product brands in foods and beverages.
- Kraft is apparently the world's second largest food company, following its acquisition of Cadbury in 2010.
- DuPont and Monsanto Company are the leading producers of pesticide, seeds, and other farming products.
- Both Archer Daniels Midland and Cargill process grain into animal feed and a diverse group of products. ADM also provides agricultural storage and transportation services, while Cargill operates a finance wing.
- Bunge is a global soybean exporter and is also involved in food processing, grain trading, and fertilizer.
- Dole Food Company is the world's largest fruit company. Chiquita Brands International, another U.S. based fruit company, is the leading distributor of bananas in the United States. Sunkist Growers, Incorporated is a U.S. based grower's cooperative.
- JBS S.A. is the world's largest processor and marketer of chicken, beef, and pork. Smithfield Foods is the world's largest pork processor and hog producer.
- Sysco Corporation, mainly catering to North America, is one of the world's largest food distributors.
- General Mills is the world's sixth biggest food manufacturing company.
- Grupo Bimbo is one of the most important baking companies in brand and trademark positioning, sales, and production volume around the world.

8 Food Technology

Food technology, or food tech for short is the application of food science to the selection, preservation, processing, packaging, distribution, and use of safe, nutritious, and wholesome food.

Food scientists and food technologists study the physical, microbiological, and chemical make-up of food. Depending on their area of specialization, food scientists may develop ways to process, preserve, package, or store food, according to industry and government specifications and regulations. Consumers seldom think of the vast array of foods and the research and development that has resulted in the means to deliver tasty, nutritious, safe, and convenient foods.

Food technology is part of the curriculum and teaches, alongside how to cook, nutrition and the food manufacturing process.

Research in the field now known as food technology has been conducted for decades. Nicolas Appert's development in 1810 of the canning process was a decisive event. The process wasn't called canning then and Appert did not really know the principle on which his process worked, but canning has had a major impact on food preservation techniques.

Louis Pasteur's research on the spoilage of wine and his description of how to avoid spoilage in 1864 was an early attempt to put food technology on a scientific basis. Besides research into wine spoilage, Pasteur did research on the production of alcohol, vinegar, wines and beer, and the souring of milk. He developed pasteurization—the process of heating milk and milk products to destroy food spoilage and disease-producing organisms. In his research into food technology, Pasteur became the pioneer into bacteriology and of modern preventive medicine.

By 1940's to 1950's, the original four departments that had taught the subject under different names (including those at the University of Massachusetts and the University of California) had been retitled 'food science', 'food science and technology', or a similar variant.

Developments in Food Technology

Several companies in the food industry have played a role in the development of food technology. These developments have contributed greatly to the food supply. Some of these developments are:

- *Instantized Milk Powder:* D.D. Peebles (U.S. patent 2,835,586) developed the first instant milk powder, which has become the basis for a variety of new products that are rehydratable in cold water or milk. This process increases the surface area of the powdered product by partially rehydrating spray-dried milk powder.
- *Freeze Drying:* The first application of freeze drying was most likely in the pharmaceutical industry; however, a successful large-scale industrial application of the process was the development of continuous freeze drying of coffee.
- *High-Temperature Short Time Processing:* These processes for the most part are characterized by rapid heating and cooling, holding for a short time at a relatively high temperature and filling aseptically into sterile containers.
- *Decaffeination of Coffee and Tea:* Decaffeinated coffee and tea was first developed on a commercial basis in Europe around 1900. The process is described in U.S. patent

897,763. Green coffee beans are treated with steam or water to around 20 per cent moisture. The added water and heat separate the caffeine from the bean to its surface. Solvents are then used to remove the caffeine from the beans. In the 1980s, new non-organic solvent techniques have been developed for the decaffeination of coffee and tea. Carbon dioxide under supercritical conditions is one of these new techniques. U.S. patent 4,820,537 was issued to General Foods Corp. for a CO_2 decaffeination process.

- *Process optimization:* Food Technology now allows production of foods to be more efficient, oil saving technologies are now available on different forms. Production methods and methodology have also become increasingly sophisticated.

Public Health

Public health is "the science and art of preventing disease, prolonging life and promoting health through the organized efforts and informed choices of society, organizations, public and private, communities and individuals" (1920, C.E.A. Winslow). It is concerned with threats to the overall health of a community based on population health analysis. The population in question can be as small as a handful of people or as large as all the inhabitants of several continents (for instance, in the case of a pandemic). Public health is typically divided into epidemiology, biostatistics and health services. Environmental, social, behavioural, and occupational health are other important subfields.

The focus of public health intervention is to prevent rather than treat a disease through surveillance of cases and the promotion of healthy behaviours. In addition to these activities, in many cases treating a disease may be vital to preventing it in others, such as during an outbreak of an infectious disease. Hand washing, vaccination programmes and distribution of condoms are examples of public health measures.

The goal of public health is to improve lives through the prevention and treatment of disease. The United Nations' World Health Organization defines health as "a state of complete physical, mental and social well-being and not merely the absence of disease or infirmity".

Most countries have their own government public health agencies, sometimes known as ministries of health, to respond to domestic health issues. In the United States, the front line of public health initiatives are state and local health departments. The United States Public Health Service (PHS), led by the Surgeon General of the United States, and the Centres for Disease Control and Prevention, headquartered in Atlanta, are involved with several international health activities, in addition to their national duties.

There is a vast discrepancy in access to health care and public health initiatives between developed nations and developing nations. In the developing world, public health infrastructures are still forming. There may not be enough trained health workers or monetary resources to provide even a basic level of medical care and disease prevention. As a result, a large majority of disease and mortality in the developing world results from and contributes to extreme poverty. For example, many African governments spend less than USD$10 per person per year on health care, while, in the United States, the federal government spent approximately USD$4,500 per capita in 2000.

Many diseases are preventable through simple, non-medical methods. For example, research has shown that the simple act of hand washing can prevent many contagious diseases.

Public health plays an important role in disease prevention efforts in both the developing world and in developed countries, through local health systems and through international non-governmental organizations.

The two major postgraduate professional degrees related to this field are the Master of Public Health (MPH) or MSc in

Public Health or allied fields. Doctoral studies in this field include Doctor of Public Health (DrPH) and PhD in a subspeciality of greater Public Health disciplines. DrPH is regarded as a leadership degree and Ph.D., is more an academic degree.

History of Public Health

In some ways, public health is a modern concept, although it has roots in antiquity. From the beginnings of human civilization, it was recognized that polluted water and lack of proper waste disposal spread communicable diseases (theory of miasma). Early religions attempted to regulate behaviour that specifically related to health, from types of food eaten, to regulating certain indulgent behaviours, such as drinking alcohol or sexual relations. The establishment of governments placed responsibility on leaders to develop public health policies and programmes in order to gain some understanding of the causes of disease and thus ensure social stability prosperity, and maintain order.

The term 'healthy city' used by today's public health advocates reflects this ongoing challenge to collective physical well-being that results from crowded conditions and urbanization.

By Roman times, it was well understood that proper diversion of human waste was a necessary tenet of public health in urban areas. The Chinese developed the practice of variolation following a smallpox epidemic around 1000 BC. An individual without the disease could gain some measure of immunity against it by inhaling the dried crusts that formed around lesions of infected individuals. Also, children were protected by inoculating a scratch on their forearms with the pus from a lesion. This practice was not documented in the West until the early-18th century, and was used on a very limited basis. The practice of vaccination did not become prevalent until the 1820s, following the work of Edward Jenner to treat smallpox.

During the 14th century Black Death in Europe, it was believed that removing bodies of the dead would further prevent the spread of the bacterial infection. This did little to stem the plague, however, which was most likely spread by rodent-borne fleas. Burning parts of cities resulted in much greater benefit, since it destroyed the rodent infestations. The development of quarantine in the mediaeval period helped mitigate the effects of other infectious diseases. However, according to Michel Foucault, the plague model of governmentality was later controverted by the cholera model. A Cholera pandemic devastated Europe between 1829 and 1851, and was first fought by the use of what Foucault called 'social medicine', which focussed on flux, circulation of air, location of cemeteries, etc. All those concerns, born of the miasma theory of disease, were mixed with urbanistic concerns for the management of populations, which Foucault designated as the concept of 'biopower'. The German conceptualized this in the *Polizeiwissenschaft* ("Science of police").

The science of epidemiology was founded by John Snow's identification of a polluted public water well as the source of an 1854 cholera outbreak in London. Dr. Snow believed in the germ theory of disease as opposed to the prevailing miasma theory. Although miasma theory correctly teaches that disease is a result of poor sanitation, it was based upon the prevailing theory of spontaneous generation. Germ theory developed slowly: despite Anton van Leeuwenhoek's observations of Microorganisms, (which are now known to cause many of the most common infectious diseases) in the year 1680, the modern era of public health did not begin until the 1880s, with Louis Pasteur's germ theory and production of artificial vaccines.

Other public health interventions include latrinization, the building of sewers, the regular collection of garbage followed by incineration or disposal in a landfill, providing clean water and draining standing water to prevent the breeding of mosquitoes. This contribution was made by Edwin

Chadwick in 1843 who published a report on the sanitation of the working class population in Great Britain at the time. So began the inception of the modern public health. The industrial revolution had initially caused the spread of disease through large conurbations around workhouses and factories. These settlements were cramped and primitive and there was no organised sanitation. Disease was inevitable and its incubation in these areas was encouraged by the poor lifestyle of the inhabitants.

Modern Public Health

As the prevalence of infectious diseases in the developed world decreased through the 20th century, public health began to put more focus on chronic diseases such as cancer and heart disease. An emphasis on physical exercise was reintroduced.

In America, public health worker Dr. Sara Josephine Baker lowered the infant mortality rate using preventative methods. She established many programmes to help the poor in New York City keep their infants healthy. Dr. Baker led teams of nurses into the crowded neighbourhoods of Hell's Kitchen and taught mothers how to dress, feed, and bathe their babies. After World War I many states and countries followed her example in order to lower infant mortality rates.

During the 20th century, the dramatic increase in average life span is widely credited to public health achievements, such as vaccination programmes and control of infectious diseases, effective safety policies such as motor-vehicle and occupational safety, improved family planning, chlorination of drinking water, smoke-free measures, and programmes designed to decrease chronic disease. One of the major sources of the increase in average life span in the early 20th century was the decline in the 'urban penalty' brought on by the improvement in water sanitation. These improvements included chlorination, filtration and sewage treatment which led to the decline in deaths caused by infectious water-diseases such as tuberculosis, cholera, diphtheria, yellow fever, smallpox, and intestinal diseases. In Cutler and Miller's, "The

Role of Public Health Improvements in Health Advances", they display evidence of the decline in typhoid fever deaths in Chicago, Baltimore, Cincinnati, and Cleveland after these cities adopted chlorination, filtration, or a sewage improvement.

Meanwhile, the developing world remained plagued by largely preventable infectious diseases, exacerbated by malnutrition and poverty. Front-page headlines continue to present society with public health issues on a daily basis: emerging infectious diseases such as SARS, making its way from China to Canada and the United States; prescription drug benefits under public programs such as Medicare; the increase of HIV-AIDS among young heterosexual women and its spread in South Africa; the increase of childhood obesity and the concomitant increase in type II diabetes among children; the impact of adolescent pregnancy; and the ongoing social, economic and health disasters related to the 2004 Tsunami and Hurricane Katrina in 2005. These are all ongoing public health challenges.

Since the 1980s, the growing field of population health has broadened the focus of public health from individual behaviours and risk factors to population-level issues such as inequality, poverty, and education. Modern public health is often concerned with addressing determinants of health across a population, rather than advocating for individual behaviour change. There is a recognition that our health is affected by many factors including where we live, genetics, our income, our educational status and our social relationships — these are known as "social determinants of health." A social gradient in health runs through society, with those that are poorest generally suffering the worst health. However even those in the *middle classes* will generally have worse health outcomes than those of a higher social stratum. The *new* public health seeks to address these health inequalities by advocating for population-based policies that improve health in an equitable manner.

Schools of Public Health

In the United States, the Welch-Rose Report of 1915 has been viewed as the basis for the critical movement in the history of the institutional schism between public health and medicine because it led to the establishment of schools of public health supported by the Rockefeller Foundation. The report was authored by William Welch, founding dean of the Johns Hopkins Bloomberg School of Public Health, and Wycliffe Rose of the Rockefeller Foundation. The report focussed more on research than practical education. Some have blamed the Rockefeller Foundation's 1916 decision to support the establishment of schools of public health for creating the schism between public health and medicine and legitimizing the rift between medicine's laboratory investigation of the mechanisms of disease and public health's nonclinical concern with environmental and social influences on health and wellness.

Even though schools of public health had already been established in Europe and North Africa, the US had still maintained the traditional system of housing faculties of public health within their medical institutions. However, a year following the Welch-Rose report, the Johns Hopkins School of Hygiene and Public Health was founded in 1916. By 1922, schools of public health were established in Columbia, Harvard and Yale universities. By 1999 there were twenty nine schools of public health in the US, enrolling around fifteen thousand students.

Over the years, the types of students and training provided have also changed. In the beginning, students who enrolled in public health schools had already obtained a medical degree. However, in 1978, 69 per cent of students enrolled in public health schools had only a bachelors degree. Public health school training had evolved from a second degree for medical professionals to a primary public health degree with a focus on the six core disciplines of biostatistics, epidemiology, health services administration, health education, behavioural science and environmental health.

Education and Training

Schools of public health offer a variety of degrees which generally fall into two categories: professional or academic.

Professional degrees are oriented towards practice in public health settings. The Master of Public Health (M.P.H.), Doctor of Public Health (Dr.PH.), Doctor of Health Science (D.H.Sc.) and the Master of Health Care Administration (M.H.A.) are examples of degrees which are geared towards people who want careers as practitioners of public health in health departments, managed care and community-based organizations, hospitals and consulting firms among others. Master of Public Health (M.P.H.) degrees broadly fall into two categories, those that put more emphasis on an understanding of epidemiology and statistics as the scientific basis of public health practice and those that include a more eclectic range of methodologies. A Master of Science of Public Health (M.S.P.H.) is similar to an M.P.H. but is considered an academic degree (as opposed to a professional degree) and places more emphasis on quantitative methods and research. The same distinction can be made between the Dr.PH. and the D.H.Sc. The Dr.PH is considered a professional degree and the D.H.Sc. is an academic degree.

Academic degrees are more oriented towards those with interests in the scientific basis of public health and preventive medicine who wish to pursue careers in research, university teaching in graduate programmes, policy analysis and development, and other high-level public health positions. Examples of academic degrees are the Master of Science (M.S.), Doctor of Philosophy (Ph.D.), Doctor of Science (Sc.D.), and Doctor of Health Science (D.H.Sc.). The doctoral programmes are distinct from the M.P.H. and other professional programmes by the addition of advanced coursework and the nature and scope of a dissertation research project.

The Association of Schools of Public Health represents Council on Education for Public Health (CEPH) accredited schools of public health.

Delta Omega is the honorary society for graduate studies in public health. The society was founded in 1924 at the Johns Hopkins School of Hygiene and Public Health. Currently, there are approximately 68 chapters throughout the United States and Puerto Rico.

Today, most governments recognize the importance of public health programmes in reducing the incidence of disease, disability, and the effects of aging, although public health generally receives significantly less government funding compared with medicine. In recent years, public health programmes providing vaccinations have made incredible strides in promoting health, including the eradication of smallpox, a disease that plagued humanity for thousands of years.

An important public health issue facing the world currently is HIV/AIDS and Antibiotic resistance leading to the reemergence of diseases such as Tuberculosis.

Another major public health concern is diabetes, according to the World Health Organization, at least 171 million people worldwide suffered from diabetes. Its incidence is increasing rapidly, and it is estimated that by the year 2030, this number will double. However, in a June 2010 editorial in the medical journal *The Lancet*, the authors opined that "The fact that type 2 diabetes, a largely preventable disorder, has reached epidemic proportion is a public health humiliation.

A controversial aspect of public health is the control of tobacco smoking. Changing smoking behavior requires long term strategies, unlike the fight against communicable diseases which takes a shorter period to take effect. Furthermore, while communicable diseases have historically ranged uppermost as a global health priority, non-communicable and behaviour-related diseases have been at the bottom. Simultaneously, global and national health policy making is increasingly aligned with industrial and trade policies, and is being done hand in hand with business, thus weakening the firewalls necessary for effective regulation and normative actions both at national and global levels. Many nations have implemented major initiatives to cut smoking, such as increased taxation and bans on smoking in some or all public places. Proponents argue by presenting evidence that smoking is one of the major killers in all developed countries, and that therefore governments have a duty to reduce the death rate, both through limiting passive (second-hand) smoking and by providing fewer opportunities for smokers to smoke. Opponents say that this undermines individual freedom and personal responsibility and worry that the state may be emboldened to remove more and more choice in the name of better population health overall. However, proponents counter that inflicting disease on other people via passive smoking is not a human right, and in fact smokers are still free to smoke in their own homes.

There is also a link between public health and veterinary public health which deals with zoonotic diseases, diseases that can be transmitted from animals to humans.

Obesity is a growing problem that public health is facing. WHO's latest projections indicate that globally in 2008 approximately 1.5 billion adults (age 20+) were overweight and of these, more than 200 million men and nearly 300 million women were obese. WHO further projects that by 2015, approximately 2.3 billion adults will be overweight and more than 700 million will be obese. Nearly 43 million children under the age of 5 years were overweight globally in 2010. The U.S. is the leading country with 30.6 per cent of its population being obese. Mexico follows behind with 24.2 per cent and the United Kingdom with 23 per cent. The weighted average percentage among 30 countries is 14.1 per cent. Obesity is responsible for 325,000 deaths every year. It was considered a problem in high-income countries, but now it is on the rise in low-income countries, especially in urban settings. There are many Public Health programmes dedicated to this issue of obesity. Many of these programme's objectives is to promote a healthy diet, nutrition, and physical activity.

Applications in Healthcare

As well as seeking to improve population health through the implementation of specific population-level interventions, public health professionals also seek to improve population health by improving the contribution of medical care to life extension and quality of life.

Such improvements could be identified by assessing what need for health services existed within the population:

1. Assessing current services
2. Ascertaining requirements as expressed by professionals, public and other stakeholders
3. Identifying the most appropriate interventions
4. Considering the effect on resources
5. Agreeing and implementing any necessary changes

In addition public health professionals can improve population health through:

1. Assessing evidence of effectiveness and cost-effectiveness for proposed interventions.
2. The evaluation of healthcare to determine whether the activity in question is meeting its objectives.
3. Supporting decision making in healthcare and planning health services.

9 Food Additive

Food additives are substances added to food to preserve flavour or enhance its taste and appearance. Some additives have been used for centuries; for example, preserving food by pickling (with vinegar), salting, as with bacon, preserving sweets or using sulfur dioxide as in some wines. With the advent of processed foods in the second half of the 20th century, many more additives have been introduced, of both natural and artificial origin.

To regulate these additives, and inform consumers, each additive is assigned a unique number, termed as 'E numbers', which is used in Europe for all approved additives. This numbering scheme has now been adopted and extended by the Codex Alimentarius Commission to internationally identify all additives, egardless of whether they are approved for use.

E numbers are all prefixed by 'E', but countries outside Europe use only the number, whether the additive is approved in Europe or not. For example, acetic acid is written as E260 on products sold in Europe, but is simply known as additive 260 in some countries. Additive 103, alkanet, is not approved for use in Europe so does not have an E number, although it is approved for use in Australia and New Zealand. Since 1987, Australia has had an approved system of labelling for additives in packaged foods. Each food additive has to be named or numbered. The numbers are the same as in Europe, but without the prefix 'E'.

The United States Food and Drug Administration listed these items as "Generally recognized as safe" or GRAS; they are listed under both their chemical abstract services number and categories.

Food additives can be divided into several groups, although there is some overlap between them.

Acids

Food acids are added to make flavours 'sharper', and also act as preservatives and antioxidants. Common food acids include vinegar, citric acid, tartaric acid, malic acid, fumaric acid, and lactic acid.

Acidity Regulators

Acidity regulators are used to change or otherwise control the acidity and alkalinity of foods.

Anticaking Agents

Anticaking agents keep powders such as milk powder from caking or sticking.

Antifoaming Agents

Antifoaming agents reduce or prevent foaming in foods.

Antioxidants

Antioxidants such as vitamin C act as preservatives by inhibiting the effects of oxygen on food, and can be beneficial to health.

Bulking Agents

Bulking agents such as starch are additives that increase the bulk of a food without affecting its nutritional value.

Food Colouring

Colourings are added to food to replace colours lost during preparation, or to make food look more attractive.

Colour Retention Agents

In contrast to colourings, colour retention agents are used to preserve a food's existing colour.

Emulsifiers

Emulsifiers allow water and oils to remain mixed together in an emulsion, as in mayonnaise, ice cream, and homogenized milk.

Flavours

Flavours are additives that give food a particular taste or smell, and may be derived from natural ingredients or created artificially.

Flavour Enhancers

Flavour enhancers enhance a food's existing flavours. They may be extracted from natural sources (through distillation, solvent extraction, maceration, among other methods) or created artificially.

Flour Treatment Agents

Flour treatment agents are added to flour to improve its colour or its use in baking.

Glazing Agents

Glazing agents provide a shiny appearance or protective coating to foods.

Humectants

Humectants prevent foods from drying out.

Tracer Gas

Tracer gas allow for package integrity testing to prevent foods from being exposed to atmosphere, thus guaranteeing shelf life.

Preservatives

Preservatives prevent or inhibit spoilage of food due to fungi, bacteria and other microorganisms.

Stabilizers

Stabilizers, thickeners and gelling agents, like agar or pectin (used in jam for example) give foods a firmer texture. While they are not true emulsifiers, they help to stabilize emulsions.

Sweeteners

Sweeteners are added to foods for flavouring. Sweeteners other than sugar are added to keep the food energy (calories) low, or because they have beneficial effects for diabetes mellitus and tooth decay and diarrhoea.

Thickeners

Thickeners are substances which, when added to the mixture, increase its viscosity without substantially modifying its other properties.

Safety

With the increasing use of processed foods since the 19th century, there has been a great increase in the use of food additives of varying levels of safety. This has led to legislation in many countries regulating their use. For example, boric acid was widely used as a food preservative from the 1870s to the 1920s, but was banned after World War I due to its toxicity, as demonstrated in animal and human studies. During World War II the urgent need for cheap, available food preservatives led to it being used again, but it was finally banned in the 1950s. Such cases led to a general mistrust of food additives, and an application of the precautionary principle led to the conclusion that only additives that are known to be safe should be used in foods. In the USA, this led to the adoption of the Delaney clause, an amendment to the Federal Food, Drug, and Cosmetic Act of 1938, stating that no carcinogenic substances may be used as food additives. However, after the banning of cyclamates in the USA and Britain in 1969, saccharin, the only remaining legal artificial sweetener at the time, was found to cause cancer in rats. Widespread public outcry in the USA, partly communicated to Congress by postage-paid postcards supplied in the packaging of sweetened soft drinks, led to the retention of saccharin despite its violation of the Delaney clause.

In September 2007, research financed by Britain's Food Standards Agency and published online by the British medical journal *The Lancet*, presented evidence that a mix of additives commonly found in children's foods increases the mean level of hyperactivity. The team of researchers concluded that "the finding lends strong support for the case that food additives exacerbate hyperactive behaviours (inattention, impulsivity and overactivity) at least into middle childhood." That study examined the effect of artificial colours and a sodium benzoate preservative, and found both to be problematic for some children. Further studies are needed to find out whether there are other additives that could have a similar effect, and it is unclear whether some disturbances can also occur in mood and concentration in some adults. In the February 2008 issue of its publication, *AAP Grand Rounds*, the American Academy of Paediatrics concluded that a low-additive diet is a valid intervention for children with ADHD.

"Although quite complicated, this was a carefully conducted study in which the investigators went to great lengths to eliminate bias and to rigorously measure outcomes. The results are hard to follow and somewhat inconsistent. For many of the assessments there were small but statistically significant differences of measured behaviours in children who consumed the food additives compared with those who did not. In each case increased hyperactive behaviours were associated with consuming the additives. For those comparisons in which no statistically significant differences were found, there was a trend for more hyperactive behaviours associated with the food additive drink in virtually every assessment. Thus, the overall findings of the study are clear and require that even we skeptics, who have long doubted parental claims of the effects of various foods on the behaviour of their children, admit we might have been wrong".

In 2007, Food Standards Australia New Zealand published an official shoppers' guidance with which the concerns of food additives and their labelling are mediated.

There has been significant controversy associated with the risks and benefits of food additives. Some artificial food additives have been linked with cancer, digestive problems, neurological conditions, ADHD, heart disease or obesity. Natural additives may be similarly harmful or be the cause of allergic reactions in certain individuals. For example, safrole was used to flavour root beer until it was shown to be carcinogenic. Due to the application of the Delaney clause, it may not be added to foods, even though it occurs naturally in sassafras and sweet basil.

Blue 1, Blue 2, Red 3, and Yellow 6 are among the food colourings that have been linked to various health risks. Blue 1 is used to colour candy, soft drinks, and pastries and there has been some evidence that it may cause cancer. Blue 2 can be found in pet food, soft drinks, and pastries, and has shown to cause brain tumours in mice. Red 3, mainly used in cherries for cocktails has been correlated with thyroid tumours in rats and humans as well. Yellow 6, used in sausages, gelatin, and candy can lead to the attribution of gland and kidney tumours and contains carcinogens, but in minimal amounts.

LIST OF FOOD ADDITIVE TYPES

Food additives can be divided into several groups, although there is some overlap between them.

Acids

Food acids are added to make flavours 'sharper', and also act as preservatives and antioxidants. Common food acids include vinegar, citric acid, tartaric acid, malic acid, fumaric acid, and lactic acid.

Acidity Regulators

Acidity regulators are used to change or otherwise control the acidity and alkalinity of foods.

Anticaking Agents

Anticaking agents keep powders such as milk powder from caking or sticking.

Antifoaming Agents

Antifoaming agents reduce or prevent foaming in foods.

Antioxidants

Antioxidants such as vitamin C act as preservatives by inhibiting the effects of oxygen on food, and can be beneficial to health.

Bulking Agents

Bulking agents such as starch are additives that increase the bulk of a food without affecting its nutritional value.

Food Colouring

Colourings are added to food to replace colours lost during preparation, or to make food look more attractive.

Colour Retention Agents

In contrast to colourings, colour retention agents are used to preserve a food's existing colour.

Emulsifiers

Emulsifiers allow water and oils to remain mixed together in an emulsion, as in mayonnaise, ice cream, and homogenized milk.

Flavours

Flavours are additives that give food a particular taste or smell, and may be derived from natural ingredients or created artificially.

Flavour Enhancers

Flavour enhancers enhance a food's existing flavours. They may be extracted from natural sources (through distillation, solvent extraction, maceration, among other methods) or created artificially.

Flour Treatment Agents

Flour treatment agents are added to flour to improve its colour or its use in baking.

Glazing Agents

Glazing agents provide a shiny appearance or protective coating to foods.

Humectants

Humectants prevent foods from drying out.

Tracer Gas

Tracer gas allow for package integrity testing to prevent foods from being exposed to atmosphere, thus guaranteeing shelf life.

Preservatives

Preservatives prevent or inhibit spoilage of food due to fungi, bacteria and other microorganisms.

Stabilizers

Stabilizers, thickeners and gelling agents, like agar or pectin (used in jam for example) give foods a firmer texture. While they are not true emulsifiers, they help to stabilize emulsions.

Sweeteners

Sweeteners are added to foods for flavouring. Sweeteners other than sugar are added to keep the food energy (calories) low, or because they have beneficial effects for diabetes mellitus and tooth decay and diarrhoea.

Thickeners

Thickeners are substances which, when added to the mixture, increase its viscosity without substantially modifying its other properties.

Caffeine and other GRAS (generally recognized as safe) additives such as sugar and salt are not required to go through the regulation process.

ALPHABETICAL INDEX OF FOOD ADDITIVES

A

Abietic acid

Acacia vera

Acacia

Acesulfame potassium - artificial sweetener

Acesulfame

Acetic acid - acidity regulator

Acetic acid esters of mono- and diglycerides of fatty acids - emulsifier

Acetylated distarch adipate - thickener, vegetable gum

Acetylated distarch phosphate - thickener, vegetable gum

Acetylated oxidised starch - thickener, vegetable gum

Acetylated starch - thickener, vegetable gum

Acid treated starch - thickener, vegetable gum

Adipic acid - food acid

Agar - thickener, vegetable gum, stabilizer, gelling agent

Alcohol

Alfalfa

Alginic acid - thickener, vegetable gum, stabilizer, gelling agent, emulsifier

Alitame - artificial sweetener

Alkaline treated starch - thickener, vegetable gum

Alkanet - colour (red)

Allspice

Allura red AC - colour (FDA: FD&C Red #40)

Almond oil - used as a substitute for olive oil. Also used as an emollient

Aluminium - colour (silver)

Aluminium ammonium sulfate - mineral salt

Aluminium potassium sulfate - mineral salt

Aluminium silicate - anti-caking agent
Aluminium sodium sulfate - mineral salt
Aluminium sulfate - mineral salt
Amaranth - colour (red) Note that amaranth dye is unrelated to the amaranth plant
Amaranth oil - high in squalene and unsaturated fatty acids - used in food and cosmetic industries
Amchur (mango powder)
Ammonium acetate - preservative, acidity regulator
Ammonium adipates - acidity regulator
Ammonium alginate - thickener, vegetable gum, stabilizer, gelling agent, emulsifier
Ammonium bicarbonate - mineral salt
Ammonium carbonate - mineral salt
Ammonium chloride - mineral salt
Ammonium ferric citrate - food acid
Ammonium fumarate - food acid
Ammonium hydroxide - mineral salt
Ammonium lactate - food acid
Ammonium malate - food acid
Ammonium phosphates - mineral salt
Ammonium phosphatides - emulsifier
Ammonium polyphosphates - anti-caking agent
Ammonium sulfate - mineral salt, improving agent
Amylases - flour treatment agent
Angelica (*Angelica archangelica*)
Anise
Annatto - colour
Anthocyanins - colour
Apricot oil - a cooking oil from certain cultivars
Arabinogalactan - thickener, vegetable gum
Argan oil - a food oil from Morocco that has also attracted recent attention in Europe

Argon - propellant

Rocket (Arugula)

Asafoetida

Ascorbic acid (Vitamin C) - antioxidant (water soluble)

Ascorbyl palmitate - antioxidant (fat soluble)

Ascorbyl stearate - antioxidant (fat soluble)

Aspartame - artificial sweetener

Astaxanthin - colour

Avocado oil - used a substitute for olive oil. Also used in cosmetics and skin care products

Azodicarbonamide - flour bleaching agent. Also used in the production of foamed plastics and the manufacture of gaskets. Banned as a food additive in Australia and Europe.

Azorubine - colour (red)

B

Babassu oil - similar to, and used as a substitute for coconut oil

Baking powder - leavening agent; includes acid and base

Baking soda - food base

Balm, lemon

Balm oil

Balsam Peru

Barberry

Barley flour

Basil (*Ocimum basilicum*)

Basil extract

Bay leaves

Beeswax - glazing agent

Beet red - colour (red)

Beetroot red - colour (red)

Ben oil - extracted from the seeds of the moringa oleifera.

High in behenic acid. Extremely stable edible oil. Also suitable for biofuel.

Bentonite - anti-caking agent

Benzoic acid - preservative

Benzoyl peroxide - flour treatment agent

Berebere

Bergamot - in Earl Grey tea

Bergamot (*Monarda didyma*)

Beta-apo-8′-carotenal (C 30) - colour

Beta-apo-8′-carotenic acid ethyl ester - colour

Betanin - colour (red)

Biphenyl - preservative

Bison grass (*Hierochloe odorata*)

Bixin - colour

Black 7984 - colour (brown and black)

Black cardamom

Black cumin

Blackcurrant seed oil - used as a food supplement, because of high content of omega-3 and omega-6 fatty acids. Also used in cosmetics.

Black limes

Black PN - colour (brown and black)

Bleached starch - thickener, vegetable gum

Bolivian Coriander (*Porophyllum ruderale*)

Bone phosphate - anti-caking agent

Borage (*Borago officinalis*)

Borage seed oil - similar to blackcurrant seed oil - used primarily medicinally

Borax - preservative

Boric acid - preservative

Brilliant Black BN- colour (brown and black)

Brilliant blue FCF - colour

Brilliant Scarlet 4R - colour

Brominated vegetable oil - emulsifier, stabiliser

Brown FK - colour (brown and black)

Bush tomato

Butane - propellant

Butylated hydroxyanisole (BHA) - antioxidant (fat soluble)

Butylated hydroxytoluene (BHT) - antioxidant (fat soluble)

C

Cacao shell

Cachou extract

Cactus root extract

Cadinene

Caffeine - stimulant

Cajeput oil

Calamus

Calcium 5′-ribonucleotides - flavour enhancer

Calcium acetate - preservative, acidity regulator

Calcium alginate - thickener, vegetable gum, stabilizer, gelling agent, emulsifier

Calcium ascorbate - antioxidant (water soluble)

Calcium aluminosilicate (calcium aluminium silicate) - anti-caking agent

Calcium ascorbate (Vitamin C)

Calcium benzoate - preservative

Calcium bisulfite - preservative, antioxidant

Calcium carbonates - colour (white), anticaking agent, stabiliser

Calcium chloride - mineral salt

Calcium citrates - food acid, firming agent

Calcium diglutamate - flavour enhancer

Calcium disodium EDTA - preservative
Calcium ferrocyanide - anti-caking agent
Calcium formate - preservative
Calcium fumarate - food acid
Calcium gluconate - acidity regulator
Calcium guanylate - flavour enhancer
Calcium hydrogen sulfite - preservative, antioxidant
Calcium hydroxide - mineral salt
Calcium inosinate - flavour enhancer
Calcium lactate - food acid
Calcium lactobionate - stabilizer
Calcium malates - food acid
Calcium oxide - mineral salt
Calcium pantothenate (Vitamin B_5)
Calcium peroxide
Calcium phosphates - mineral salt, anti-caking agent, firming agent
Calcium polyphosphates - anti-caking agent
Calcium propionate - preservative
Calcium salts of fatty acids - emulsifier, stabiliser, anti-caking agent
Calcium silicate - anti-caking agent
Calcium sorbate - preservative
Calcium stearoyl lactylate - emulsifier
Calcium sulfate - flour treatment agent, mineral salt, sequestrant, improving agent, firming agent
Calcium sulfite - preservative, antioxidant
Calcium tartrate - food acid, emulsifier
Camomile -
Candelilla wax - glazing agent
Candle nut

Canola oil/Rapeseed oil, one of the most widely used cooking oil, from a (trademarked) cultivar of rapeseed.

Canthaxanthin - colour

Caper (*Capparis spinosa*)

Capsanthin - colour

Capsorubin - colour

Carrageenan - A family of linear sulphated polysaccharides extracted from red seaweeds

Caramel I (plain) - colour (brown and black)

Caramel II Caustic Sulfite process) - colour (brown and black)

Caramel III Ammonia process) - colour (brown and black)

Caramel IV (Ammonia sulfite process) - colour (brown and black)

Caraway

Carbamide - flour treatment agent

Carbon black - colour (brown and black)

Carbon dioxide - acidity regulator, propellant

Cardamom

Carmines - colour (red)

Carmoisine - colour (red)

Carnauba wax - glazing agent

Carob Pod

Carob pod oil/Algaroba oil, used medicinally

Carotenes - colour

Carotene - Alpha - colour

Carotene -Beta - colour

Carotene - Gamma - colour

Carrageenan - thickener, vegetable gum, stabilizer, gelling agent, emulsifier

Carrot oil

Cashew oil - somewhat comparable to olive oil. May have value for fighting dental cavities

Cassia
Catechu extract
Celery salt
Celery seed
Chalk - colour (white), anticaking agent, stabiliser
Chervil (*Anthriscus cerefolium*)
Chicory
Chicory Root Extract - High in inulin
Chile pepper
Chili powder
Chives (*Allium schoenoprasum*)
Chlorine dioxide - flour treatment agent
Chlorine - flour treatment agent
Chlorophylls and Chlorophyllins - colour (green)
Chocolate Brown HT - colour
Choline salts and esters - emulsifier
Chrysoine resorcinol - colour (red)
Cicely (*Myrrhis odorata*)
Cicely sweet (*Myrrhis odorata*)
Cilantro
Cinnamon
Cinnamon oil - used for flavouring
Citranaxanthin - colour
Citric acid - food acid
Citric acid esters of mono- and diglycerides of fatty acids - emulsifier
Citrus red 2 - colour (red)
Cloves
Cochineal - colour (red)
Coconut oil - a cooking oil, high in saturated fat - particularly used in baking and cosmetics
Copper complexes of chlorophylls - colour (green)

Coriander

Coriander seed oil - used medicinally. Also used as a flavouring agent in pharmaceutical and food industries

Corn oil - one of the most common, and inexpensive cooking oils

Corn syrup

Costmary

Cottonseed oil - a major food oil, often used in industrial food processing.

Cress

Crocetin - colour

Crocin - colour

Crosslinked sodium carboxymethylcellulose - emulsifier

Cryptoxanthin - colour

Cumin

Cumin oil/Black seed oil - used as a flavour, particularly in meat products. Also used in veterinary medicine

Cupric sulfate - mineral salt

Curcumin - colour (yellow and orange)

Curry powder

Curry leaf (*Murraya koenigii*)

Cyanocobalamin (Vitamin B12)

Cyclamates - artificial sweetener

Cyclamic acid - artificial sweetener

Cyclodextrin beta - emulsifier

D

Damiana (*Turnera aphrodisiaca, T. diffusa*)

Dandelion leaf

Dandelion Root

Dandelion (*Taraxacum officinale*)

Decanal dimethyl acetal

Decanal

Decanoic acid

Dehydroacetic acid - preservative

Delta-tocopherol(synthetic) - antioxidant

Devil's claw (*Harpagophytum procumbens*) medicinal

Dextrin roasted starch - thickener, vegetable gum

Diacetyltartaric acid esters of mono- and diglycerides of fatty acids - emulsifier

Dicalcium diphosphate - anti-caking agent

Dilauryl thiodipropionate - antioxidant

Dill seed

Dill (*Anethum graveolens*)

Dimethyl dicarbonate - preservative

Dimethylpolysiloxane - emulsifier, anti-caking agent

Dioctyl sodium sulfosuccinate - emulsifier

Diphenyl - preservative

Diphosphates - mineral salt, emulsifier

Dipotassium guanylate - flavour enhancer

Dipotassium inosinate - flavour enhancer

Disodium 5'-ribonucleotides - flavour enhancer

Disodium ethylenediaminetetraacetate - antioxidant, preservative

Disodium guanylate - flavour enhancer

Disodium inosinate - flavour enhancer

Distarch phosphate - thickener, vegetable gum

Distearyl thiodipropionate - antioxidant

Dl-alpha-tocopherol (synthetic) - antioxidant

Dodecyl gallate - antioxidant

E

Echinacea

EDTA - Antioxidant, Chelating Agent

Egg

Egg yolk

Egg white

Elderberry

Eleutherococcus senticosus

Enzymatically hydrolyzed Carboxymethyl cellulose - emulsifier

Enzyme treated starch - thickener, vegetable gum

Epazote (*Chenopodium ambrosioides*)

Epsom salts - mineral salt, acidity regulator, firming agent

Erythorbin acid - antioxidant

Erythrosine - colour (red)

Erythritol - artificial sweetener

Ethanol (alcohol)

Ethyl maltol - flavour enhancer

Ethyl methyl cellulose - thickener, vegetable gum, emulsifier

Ethylparaben (ethyl para-hydroxybenzoate) - preservative

Ethylenediamine tetraacetic acid

Evening primrose (*Oenothera biennis* et al.)

Evening primrose oil - used as a food supplement for its purported medicinal properties

F

False flax oil made of the seeds

Fantesk

Farnesol

Fast green FCF - colour

Fat

Favoxanthin - colour

Fennel (*Foeniculum vulgare*)

Fenugreek
Ferric ammonium citrate - food acid
Ferrous gluconate - colour retention agent
Ferrous lactate
Filé powder
Five-spice powder (Chinese)
Fo-ti-tieng
Formaldehyde - preservative
Formic acid - preservative
Fructose
Fumaric acid - acidity regulator

G

Galangal
Galangal root
Galbanum oil
Gallic acid
Gamma-tocopherol (synthetic) - antioxidant
Garam masala
Garlic extract
Garlic
Garlic oil
Gelatin/gelatine - Gelling agent, emulsifier
Gellan gum - thickener, vegetable gum, stabilizer, emulsifier
Ginger
Ginger oil
Ginger root
Ginseng
Glacial Acetic acid - preservative, acidity regulator
Glucitol
Gluconate

Glucono delta-lactone - acidity regulator

Glucose oxidase - antioxidant

Glucose syrup - sweetener

Glutamate

Glutamic acid - flavour enhancer

Gluten

Glycerin - humectant, sweetener

Glycerol

Glycerol ester of wood rosin - emulsifier

Glyceryl distearate - emulsifier

Glyceryl monostearate - emulsifier

Glycine - flavour enhancer

Glyoxylic acid

Gold - colour (gold)

Grains of paradise

Grape colour extract

Grape seed oil - suitable for cooking at high temperatures. also used as a salad oil, and in cosmetics

Green S - colour (green)

Green tea

Guanylic acid - flavour enhancer

Guar gum - thickener, vegetable gum, stabilizer

Guaranine

Gum acacia - thickener, vegetable gum, stabilizer, emulsifier

Gum arabic - thickener, vegetable gum, stabilizer, emulsifier

Gum guaicum - preservative

H

Haw bark

Hazelnut oil - used for its flavour. Also used in skin care, because of its slight astringent nature

Heliotropin
Helium - propellant
Hemlock oil
Hemp oil - a high quality food oil
Heptyl p-hydroxybenzoate - preservative
Hesperidin
Hexamine (hexamethylene tetramine) - preservative
Hexyl acetate
High fructose corn syrup
Horseradish
Hydrochloric acid - acidity regulator
Hydroxypropyl cellulose - thickener, vegetable gum, emulsifier
Hydroxypropyl distarch phosphate - thickener, vegetable gum
Hydroxypropyl methylcellulose - thickener, vegetable gum, emulsifier
Hydroxypropyl starch - thickener, vegetable gum
Hyssop (*Hyssopus officinalis*)

I

Indanthrene blue RS - colour (blue)
Indigo carmine - colour (blue)
Indigotine - colour (blue)
Indole
Inosinate
Inosinic acid - flavour enhancer
Inositol
Insoluble fiber
Intense sweeteners
Inulin
Invert sugar

Invertase

Iron ammonium citrate

Iron

Iron oxides and hydroxides - colour

Isobutane - propellant

Isomalt - humectant

Isopropyl citrates - antioxidant, preservative

J

Jasmine

Jamaican jerk spice

Jasmine absolute

Jiaogulan (*Gynostemma pentaphyllum*)

Juniper

Juniper berry

Juniper berry oil - used as a flavour. Also used medicinally, including traditional medicine

Juniper extract

K

Kaffir Lime Leaves (*Citrus hystrix, C. papedia*)

Kaolin - anti-caking agent

Kapok seed oil - used as an edible oil, and in soap production

Karaya gum - thickener, vegetable gum, stabilizer, emulsifier

Kelp

Kokam

Kola nut extract

Konjac - thickener, vegetable gum

Konjac glucomannate - thickener, vegetable gum

Konjac gum - thickener, vegetable gum

L

L-cysteine - flour treatment agent

Lactic acid - acidity regulator, preservative, antioxidant

Lactic acid esters of mono- and diglycerides of fatty acids - emulsifier

Lactitol - humectant

Lactose

Lactylated fatty acid esters of glycerol and propylene glycol - emulsifier

Larch gum

Lard

Latolrubine - colour

Laurel berry

Laurel leaf oil

Lavender (*Lavandula spp.*)

Lavender oil

Lecithins - antioxidant, Emulsifier

Lecithin citrate - preservative

Legume

Lemon

Lemon balm (*Melissa officinalis*)

Lemon extract

Lemon juice

Lemongrass (*Cymbopogon citratus, C. flexuosus*, and other species)

Lemon Myrtle (*Backhousia citriodora*)

Lemon oil

Lemon verbena (*Lippia citriodora*)

Lemongrass Oil

Leucine - flavour enhancer

Licorice

Lipases - flavour enhancer

Lithol Rubine BK - colour

Litholrubine - colour

Locust bean gum - thickener, vegetable gum, stabilizer, gelling agent, emulsifier

Long pepper

Lovage (*Levisticum officinale*)

L(+)- Tartaric acid - food acid

Lutein - colour

Luohanguo

Lycopene - colour

Lysine

Lysozyme - preservative

M

Macadamia oil - used as an edible oil. Also used as a massage oil

Mace

Magnesium

Magnesium carbonate - anti-caking agent, mineral salt

Magnesium chloride - mineral salt

Magnesium citrate - acidity regulator

Magnesium diglutamate - flavour enhancer

Magnesium hydroxide - mineral salt

Magnesium lactate - food acid

Magnesium oxide - anti-caking agent

Magnesium phosphates - mineral salt, anti-caking agent

Magnesium salts of fatty acids - emulsifier, stabiliser, anti-caking agent

Magnesium silicate - anti-caking agent

Magnesium stearate - emulsifier, stabiliser

Magnesium sulfate - mineral salt, acidity regulator, firming agent

Mahlab
Malabathrum
Malic acid - acidity regulator
Malt extract - flavour enhacer
Maltitol - humectant, stabiliser
Maltodextrin - carbohydrate sweetener
Maltol - flavour enhancer
Maltose
Mandarin oil-leavening agent
Manganese
Mannitol - humectant, anti-caking agent, sweetener
Margarine
Marjoram (*Origanum majorana*)
Mastic
Meadowfoam seed oil - highly stable oil, with over 98 per cent long-chain fatty acids. Competes with rapeseed oil for industrial applications
Mega-purple - a Kosher food additive made from grapes
Mentha arvensis oil/Mint oil, used in flavouring toothpastes, mouthwashes and pharmaceuticals, as well as in aromatherapy and other medicinal applications
Metatartaric acid - food acid, emulsifier
Methionine
Methyl butyrate
Methyl disulfide
Methyl ethyl cellulose - thickener, vegetable gum, emulsifier
Methyl hexenoate
Methyl isobutyrate
Methylcellulose - thickener, emulsifier, vegetable gum
Methylparaben (methyl para-hydroxybenzoate) - preservative
Methyltheobromine

Microcrystalline cellulose - anti-caking agent

Milk thistle (*Silybum*)

Milk

Mint (*Mentha spp.*)

Mixed acetic and tartaric acid esters of mono- and diglycerides of fatty acids - emulsifier

Modified starch

Molasses extract

Molybdenum

Mono and diglycerides of Fatty acids - emulsifier

Monoammonium glutamate - flavour enhancer

Monopotassium glutamate - flavour enhancer

Monosodium glutamate (MSG) - flavour enhancer

Monostarch phosphate - thickener, vegetable gum

Montanic acid esters - humectant

Mullein (*Verbascum thapsus*)

Mustard

Mustard oil (essential oil), containing a high percentage of allyl isothiocyanate or other isothiocyanates, depending on the species of mustard

Mustard oil (pressed) - used in India as a cooking oil. also used as a massage oil

Mustard plant

Mustard seed

N

Natamycin - preservative

Neohesperidin dihydrochalcone - artificial sweetener

Niacin (vitamin B_3) - colour retention agent

Nicotinic acid (vitamin B_3) - colour retention agent

Nicotinamide (vitamin B_3) - colour retention agent

Nigella (Kolanji, Black caraway)

Nisin - preservative

Nitrogen - propellant

Nitrous oxide - propellant

Norbixin - colour

Nutmeg

O

Octyl gallate - antioxidant

Okra oil (Hibiscus seed oil) - from the seed of the *Hibiscus esculentus*. Composed predominantly of oleic and lanoleic acids

Oleomargarine

Olive oil - used in cooking - cosmetics - soaps and as a fuel for traditional oil lamps

Orange GGN - colour (orange)

Orange oil - like lemon oil - cold pressed rather than distilled. Consists of 90 per cent d- Limonene. Used as a fragrance, in cleaning products and in flavouring foods

Orcein - colour (red)

Orchil - colour (red)

Oregano (*Origanum vulgare, O. heracleoticum*, and other species)

Oregano oil - contains thymol and carvacrol - making it a useful fungicide. Also used to treat digestive problems

Orris root

Orthophenyl phenol - preservative

Oxidised polyethylene wax - humectant

Oxidised starch - thickener, vegetable gum

Oxystearin - antioxidant, sequestrant

P

Palm oil - the most widely produced tropical oil. Also used to make biofuel

Panax ginseng

Panax quinquefolia

Ponch phoran

Pandan leaf

Pantothenic acid (Vitamin B_5)

Papain - A cysteine protease hydrolase enzyme present in papaya (Carica papaya) and mountain papaya (Vasconcellea cundinamarcensis)

Paprika red

Paprika

Paprika extract

Paraffins - glazing agent

Parsley (*Petroselinum crispum*)

Patent blue V - colour (blue)

Peanut oil/Ground nut oil - mild-flavoured cooking oil

Pecan oil - valued as a food oil, but requiring fresh pecans for good quality oil

Pectin - vegetable gum, emulsifier

Perilla seed oil - high in omega-3 fatty acids. Used as an edible oil, for medicinal purposes, in skin care products and as a drying oil

Pepper (black, white, and green)

Phosphated distarch phosphate - thickener, vegetable gum

Phosphoric acid - food acid

Phytic acid - preservative

Pigment Rubine - colour

Pimaricin - preservative

Pine needle oil

Pine seed oil - an expensive food oil, used in salads and as a condiment

Pistachio oil - strongly flavoured oil, particularly for use in salads

Prune kernel oil - marketed as a gourmet cooking oil
Poly vinyl pyrrolidone
Polydextrose - humectant
Polyethylene glycol 8000 - antifoaming agent
Polyglycerol esters of fatty acids - emulsifier
Polyglycerol polyricinoleate - emulsifier Polymethylsiloxane - antifoaming agent
Polyoxyethylene (40) stearate - emulsifier
Polyoxyethylene (8) stearate - emulsifier, stabilizer
Polyphosphates - mineral salt, emulsifier
Polysorbate 20 - emulsifier
Polysorbate 40 - emulsifier
Polysorbate 60 - emulsifier
Polysorbate 65 - emulsifier
Polysorbate 80 - emulsifier
Polyvinylpolypyrrolidone - colour stabiliser
Pomegranate seeds (though some consider these a fruit, not a spice)
Ponceau 4R - colour (FDA: Ext D&C Red #8)
Ponceau 6R - colour
Ponceau SX - colour
Poppy seed
Poppyseed oil - used for cooking, moisturizing skin, and in paints, varnishes and soaps
Potassium acetates - preservative, acidity regulator
Potassium adipate - food acid
Potassium alginate - thickener, vegetable gum, stabilizer, gelling agent, emulsifier
Potassium aluminium silicate - anti-caking agent
Potassium ascorbate - antioxidant (water soluble)
Potassium benzoate - preservative
Potassium bicarbonate - mineral salt

Potassium bisulfite - preservative, antioxidant
Potassium bromate - flour treatment agent
Potassium carbonate - mineral salt
Potassium chloride - mineral salt
Potassium citrates - food acid
Potassium ferrocyanide - anti-caking agent
Potassium fumarate - food acid
Potassium gluconate - stabiliser
Potassium hydrogen sulfite - preservative, antioxidant
Potassium hydroxide - mineral salt
Potassium lactate - food acid
Potassium malate - food acid
Potassium metabisulfite - preservative, antioxidant
Potassium nitrate - preservative, colour fixative
Potassium nitrite - preservative, colour fixative
Potassium phosphates - mineral salt
Potassium propionate - preservative
Potassium salts of fatty acids - emulsifier, stabiliser, anti-caking agent
Potassium sodium tartrate - food acid
Potassium sorbate - preservative
Potassium sulfate - mineral salt, seasoning
Potassium sulfite - preservative, antioxidant
Potassium tartrates - food acid
Powdered Cellulose - anti-caking agent
Primrose (*Primula*) - candied flowers, tea
Processed Eucheuma seaweed - thickener, vegetable gum, stabilizer, gelling agent, emulsifier
Propane-1,2-diol alginate - thickener, vegetable gum, stabilizer, emulsifier
Propionic acid - preservative
Propyl gallate - antioxidant

Propylene glycol - humectant

Propylene glycol alginate - thickener, vegetable gum, stabilizer, emulsifier

Propylene glycol esters of fatty acids - emulsifier

Propylparaben (propyl para-hydroxybenzoate) - preservative

Pumpkin seed oil - a specialty cooking oil, produced in Austria and Slovenia. Doesn't tolerate high temperatures

Pulegone

Purslane

Pyridoxine hydrochloride (Vitamin B_6)

Q

Quatre épices

Quillaia extract - humectant

Quinoa oil - similar in composition and use to corn oil

Quinoline Yellow WS - colour (yellow and orange)

R

Ramtil oil - pressed from the seeds of the one of several species of genus Guizotia abyssinica (Niger pea) in India and Ethiopia. Used for both cooking and lighting

Ras-el hanout

Raspberry (leaves)

Red 2G - colour

Refined microcrystalline wax - glazing agent

Rhodoxanthin - colour

Riboflavin (vitamin B_2) - colour (yellow and orange)

Rice bran oil - suitable for high temperature cooking. Widely used in Asia

Rosemary (*Rosmarinus officinalis*)

Rubixanthin - colour

S

Saccharin - artificial sweetener

Safflower oil - a flavourless and colourless cooking oil

Safflower

Saffron - colour

Sage (*Salvia officinalis*)

Saigon Cinnamon

Salad Burnet (*Sanguisorba minor* or *Poterium sanguisorba*)

Salt

Sandalwood - colour

Savory (*Satureja hortensis, S. montana*)

Scarlet GN - colour

Sesame oil - used as a cooking oil, and as a massage oil, particularly in India

Sesame seed

Shellac - glazing agent

Silicon dioxide - anti-caking agent

Silver - colour (silver)

Sodium acetate - preservative, acidity regulator

Sodium adipate - food acid

Sodium alginate - thickener, vegetable gum, stabilizer, gelling agent, emulsifier

Sodium aluminium phosphate - acidity regulator, emulsifier

Sodium aluminosilicate (sodium aluminium silicate) - anti-caking agent

Sodium ascorbate - antioxidant (water soluble)

Sodium benzoate - preservative

Sodium bicarbonate - mineral salt

Sodium bisulfite (sodium hydrogen sulfite) - preservative, antioxidant

Sodium carbonate - mineral salt

Sodium carboxymethylcellulose - emulsifier

Sodium citrates - food acid

Sodium dehydroacetate - preservative

Sodium erythorbate - antioxidant

Sodium erythorbin - antioxidant

Sodium ethyl para-hydroxybenzoate - preservative

Sodium ferrocyanide - anti-caking agent

Sodium formate - preservative

Sodium fumarate - food acid

Sodium gluconate - stabiliser

Sodium hydrogen acetate - preservative, acidity regulator

Sodium hydroxide - mineral salt

Sodium lactate - food acid

Sodium malates - food acid

Sodium metabisulfite - preservative, antioxidant, bleaching agent

Sodium methyl para-hydroxybenzoate - preservative

Sodium nitrate - preservative, colour fixative

Sodium nitrite - preservative, colour fixative

Sodium orthophenyl phenol - preservative

Sodium phosphates - Mineral Salt

Sodium propionate - preservative

Sodium propyl para-hydroxybenzoate - preservative

Sodium sorbate - preservative

Sodium stearoyl lactylate - emulsifier

Sodium succinates - acidity regulator, flavour enhancer

Sodium salts of fatty acids - emulsifier, stabiliser, anti-caking agent

Sodium sulfite - mineral salt, preservative, antioxidant

Sodium sulfite - preservative, antioxidant

Sodium tartrates - food acid

Sodium tetraborate - preservative

Sorbic acid - preservative
Sorbitan monolaurate - emulsifier
Sorbitan monooleate - emulsifier
Sorbitan monopalmitate - emulsifier
Sorbitan monostearate - emulsifier
Sorbitan tristearate - emulsifier
Sorbitol - humectant, emulsifier, sweetener
Sorbol
Sorrel (*Rumex spp.*)
Soybean oil - accounts for about half of worldwide edible oil production
Spearmint oil - often used in flavouring mouthwash and chewing gum, among other applications
Stannous chloride - colour retention agent, antioxidant
Star anise
Star anise oil - highly fragrant oil using in cooking. Also used in perfumery and soaps, has been used in toothpastes, mouthwashes, and skin creams. 90 per cent of the world's star anise crop is used in the manufacture of Tamiflu, a drug used to treat avian flu.
Starch sodium octenylsuccinate - thickener, vegetable gum
Stearic acid - anti-caking agent
Stearyl tartarate - emulsifier
Succinic acid - food acid
Sucralose - artificial sweetener
Sucroglycerides - emulsifier
Sucrose acetate isobutyrate - emulsifier, stabiliser
Sucrose esters of fatty acids - emulsifier
Sugar
Sulfur dioxide - preservative, antioxidant
Sulfuric acid - acidity regulator
Sumac

Sunflower oil - a common cooking oil, also used to make biodiesel

Sunset yellow FCF - colour (yellow and orange) (FDA: FD & C Yellow #6)

Sweet basil

Sweet woodruff

Szechuan pepper (*Xanthoxylum piperitum*)

T

Talc - anti-caking agent

Tamarind

Tandoori masala

Tannins - colour, emulsifier, stabiliser, thickener

Tansy

Tara gum - thickener, vegetable gum, stabilizer

Tarragon (*Artemisia dracunculus*)

Tartaric acid esters of mono- and diglycerides of fatty acids - emulsifier

Tartrazine - colour (yellow and orange) (FDA: FD & C Yellow #5)

Tea oil/Camellia oil, widely used in southern China as a cooking oil. Also used in making soaps, hair oils and a variety of other products.

Tert-butylhydroquinone - antioxidant

Tetrahydrocannabinol- flavour enhancer, potential anti carcinogen

Thaumatin - flavour enhancer, artificial sweetener

Theine

Thermally oxidised soya bean oil - emulsifier

Thiabendazole - preservative

Thiamine (Vitamin B1)

Thiodipropionic acid - antioxidant

Thyme

Titanium dioxide - colour (white)

Tocopherol (Vitamin E)

Tocopherol concentrate (natural) - antioxidant

Tragacanth - thickener, vegetable gum, stabilizer, emulsifier

Triacetin - humectant

Triammonium citrate - food acid

Triethyl citrate - thickener, vegetable gum

Trimethylxanthine

Triphosphates - mineral salt, emulsifier

Turmeric - colour (yellow and orange)

V

Vanilla (*Vanilla planifolia*)

Vegetable carbon - colour (brown and black)

Vinegar

Violaxanthin - colour

Vitamin

Vitamin A (Retinol)

Vitamin B_1 (Thiamine)

Vitamin B_2 (Riboflavin)

Vitamin B_5 (Pantothenic acid)

Vitamin B_6 (Pyrodoxine)

Vitamin B_{12} (Cyanocobalamin)

Vitamin C (Ascorbic acid)

Vitamin D (Calciferol)

Vitamin E (Tocopherol)

Vitamin K (Potassium)

W

Walnut oil - used for its flavour, also used by Renaissance painters in oil paints

Wasabi

Water

Wattleseed

Wheat germ oil - used as a food supplement, and for its 'grainy' flavour. Also used medicinally. Highly unstable

X

Xanthan gum - thickener, vegetable gum, stabilizer

Xylitol - humectant, stabiliser

Y

Yellow 2G - colour (yellow and orange)

Yucca extract

Z

Za'atar

Zeaxanthin - colour

Zinc acetate - flavour enhancer

10 Canning

Canning is a method of preserving food in which the food is processed and sealed in an airtight container, providing a typical shelf life ranging from 1 year to 5 years and under specific circumstances a freeze dried canned product can last as long as 30 years and can still be safely consumed. The process was first developed as a French military discovery by Nicolas Appert in 1810. The packaging prevents microorganisms from entering and proliferating inside.

To prevent the food from being spoiled before and during containment, quite a number of methods are used: pasteurisation, boiling (and other applications of high temperature over a period of time), refrigeration, freezing, drying, vacuum treatment, antimicrobial agents that are natural to the recipe of the foods being preserved, a sufficient dose of ionizing radiation, submersion in a strong saline solution, acid, base, osmotically extreme (for example very sugary) or other microbe-challenging environments.

Other than sterilization, no method is perfectly dependable as a preservative. For example, the microorganism *Clostridium botulinum* (which causes botulism), can only be eliminated at temperatures above the boiling point.

From a public safety point of view, foods with low acidity (a pH more than 4.6) need sterilization under high temperature (116-130°C). To achieve temperatures above the boiling point requires the use of a pressure canner. Foods that must be pressure canned include most vegetables, meats, seafood, poultry, and dairy products. The only foods that may be safely canned in an ordinary boiling water bath are highly acidic ones with a pH below 4.6, such as fruits, pickled vegetables, or other foods to which acidic additives have been added.

During the first years of the Napoleonic Wars, the French government offered a hefty cash award of 12,000 francs to any inventor who could devise a cheap and effective method of preserving large amounts of food. The larger armies of the period required increased, regular supplies of quality food. Limited food availability was among the factors limiting military campaigns to the summer and autumn months. In 1809, a French confectioner and brewer, Nicolas Appert, observed that food cooked inside a jar did not spoil unless the seals leaked, and developed a method of sealing food in glass jars. The reason for lack of spoilage was unknown at the time, since it would be another 50 years before Louis Pasteur demonstrated the role of microbes in food spoilage. However, glass containers presented challenges for transportation.

Glass jars were largely replaced in commercial canneries with cylindrical tin or wrought-iron canisters (later shortened to 'cans') following the work of Peter Durand (1810). Cans are cheaper and quicker to make, and much less fragile than glass jars. Glass jars have remained popular for some high-value products and in home canning. Can openers were not invented for another thirty years—at first, soldiers had to cut the cans open with bayonets or smash them open with rocks. The French Army began experimenting with issuing canned foods to its soldiers, but the slow process of canning foods and the even slower development and transport stages prevented the army from shipping large amounts across the French Empire, and the war ended before the process was perfected. Unfortunately for Appert, the factory which he had built with his prize money was razed in 1814 by Allied soldiers invading France. for home canning.

Following the end of the Napoleonic Wars, the canning process was gradually employed in other European countries and in the US. Based on Appert's methods of food preservation, Peter Durand patented a process in the United Kingdom in 1810. He did not develop the process, selling his patent in 1811 to Bryan Donkin and John Hall, who were in business as Donkin Hall and Gamble, of Bermondsey. Bryan Donkin developed the process of packaging food in sealed airtight cans, made of tinned wrought iron. Initially, the canning process was slow and labour-intensive, as each large can had to be hand-made, and took up to six hours to cook, making canned food too expensive for ordinary people. The main market for the food at this stage was the British Army and Royal Navy. By 1817 Donkin recorded that he had sold £3000 worth of canned meat in six months. In 1824 Sir William Edward Parry took canned beef and pea soup with him on his voyage to the Arctic in HMS Fury, during his search for a northwestern passage to India. In 1829, Admiral Sir James Ross also took canned food to the Arctic, as did Sir John Franklin in 1845. Some of his stores were found by the search expedition led by Captain (later Admiral Sir) Leopold McLintock in 1857. One of these cans was opened in 1939, and was edible and nutritious, though it was not analysed for contamination by the lead solder used in its manufacture.

Throughout the mid-19th century, canned food became a status symbol amongst middle-class households in Europe, becoming something of a frivolous novelty. Early methods of manufacture employed poisonous lead solder for sealing the cans, which may have worsened the disastrous outcome of the 1845 Franklin expedition to chart and navigate the Northwest Passage.

Increasing mechanisation of the canning process, coupled with a huge increase in urban populations across Europe, resulted in a rising demand for canned food. A number of inventions and improvements followed, and by the 1860s smaller machine-made steel cans were possible, and the time to cook food in sealed cans had been reduced from around six hours to thirty minutes. Canned food also began to spread beyond Europe—Robert Ayars established the first American canning factory in New York City in 1812, using improved tin-plated wrought-iron cans for preserving oysters, meats, fruits and vegetables. Demand for canned food greatly increased during wars. Large-scale wars in the nineteenth century, such as the Crimean War, American Civil War, and Franco-Prussian War introduced increasing numbers of working-class men to canned food, and allowed canning companies to expand their businesses to meet military demands for non-perishable food, allowing companies to manufacture in bulk and sell to wider civilian markets after wars ended. Urban populations in Victorian era Britain demanded ever-increasing quantities of cheap, varied, quality food that they could keep at home without having to go shopping daily. In response, companies such as Nestlé, Heinz, and others emerged to provide quality canned food for sale to working class city-dwellers. In particular, Crosse and Blackwell took over the concern of Donkin Hall and Gamble. The late 19th century saw the range of canned food available to urban populations greatly increase, as canners competed with each other using novel foodstuffs, highly decorated printed labels, and lower prices.

Demand for canned food skyrocketed during World War I, as military commanders sought vast quantities of cheap, high-calorie food to feed their millions of soldiers, which could be transported safely, survive trench conditions, and not spoil in transport. Throughout the war, soldiers generally subsisted on low-quality canned foodstuffs, such as the British 'Bully Beef' (cheap corned beef), pork and beans and Maconochies Irish Stew, but by 1916 widespread boredom with cheap canned food amongst soldiers resulted in militaries purchasing better-quality food to improve morale, and the complete meals in a can began to appear. In 1917 the French Army began issuing canned French cuisine, such as coq au vin, while the Italian Army experimented with canned ravioli and spaghetti bolognese. Shortages of canned food in the British Army in 1917 led to the government issuing cigarettes and amphetamines to soldiers to suppress their appetites. After the war, companies that had supplied military canned food improved the quality of their goods for civilian sale.

Today, tin-coated steel is the material most commonly used. Laminate vacuum pouches are also used for canning, such as used in MREs and Capri Sun drinks.

Invented in 1888 by Max Ams, modern double seams provide an airtight seal to the tin can. This airtight nature is crucial to keeping bacteria out of the can and keeping its contents sealed inside. Thus, double seamed cans are also known as Sanitary Cans. Developed in 1900 in Europe, this sort of can was made of the traditional cylindrical body made with tin plate. The two ends (lids) were attached using what is now called a double seam. A can thus sealed is impervious to the contamination by creating two tight continuous folds between the can's cylindrical body and the lids. This eliminated the need for solder and allowed improvements in manufacturing speed, reducing cost.

Double seaming uses rollers to shape the can, lid and the final double seam. To make a sanitary can and lid suitable for double seaming, manufacture begins with a sheet of coated tin plate. To create the can body, rectangles are cut and curled around a die, and welded together creating a cylinder with a side seam.

Rollers are then used to flare out one or both ends of the cylinder to create a quarter circle flange around the circumference. Precision is required to ensure that the welded sides are perfectly aligned, as any misalignment will cause inconsistent flange shape, compromising its integrity.

A circle is then cut from the sheet using a die cutter. The circle is shaped in a stamping press to create a downward countersink to fit snugly in to the can body. The result can be compared to an upside down and very flat top hat. The outer edge is then curled down and around about 140 degrees using rollers to create the end curl.

The result is a steel tube with a flanged edge, and a countersunk steel disc with a curled edge. A rubber compound is put inside the curl.

The body and end are brought together in a seamer and held in place by the base plate and chuck, respectively. The base plate provides a sure footing for the can body during the seaming operation and the chuck fits snugly in to the end (lid). The result is the countersink of the end sits inside the top of the can body just below the flange. The end curl protrudes slightly beyond the flange.

First Operation

Once brought together in the seamer, the seaming head presses a first operation roller against the end curl. The end curl is pressed against the flange curling it in toward the body and under the flange. The flange is also bent downward, and the end and body are now loosely joined together. The first operation roller is then retracted. At this point five thicknesses of steel exist in the seam. From the outside in they are:

- ❖ End
- ❖ Flange
- ❖ End Curl
- ❖ Body
- ❖ Counters

Second Operation

The seaming head then engages the second operation roller against the partly formed seam. The second operation presses all five steel components together tightly to form the final seal. The five layers in the final seam are then called:

(a) End
(b) Body Hook
(c) Cover Hook
(d) Body
(e) Countersink.

All sanitary cans require a filling medium within the seam because otherwise the metal-to-metal contact will not maintain a hermetic seal. In most cases, a rubberized compound is placed inside the end curl radius, forming the critical seal between the end and the body.

Probably the most important innovation since the introduction of double seams is the welded side seam. Prior to the welded side seam, the can body was folded and/or soldered together, leaving a relatively thick side seam. The thick side seam required that the side seam end juncture at the end curl to have more metal to curl around before closing in behind the Body Hook or flange, with a greater opportunity for error.

Seamer Setup and Quality Assurance

Many different parts during the seaming process are critical in ensuring that a can is airtight and vacuum sealed. The dangers of a can that is not hermetically sealed are contamination by foreign objects (bacteria or fungicide sprays), or that the can could leak or spoil.

One important part is the seamer setup. This process is usually performed by an experienced technician. Amongst the parts that need setup are seamer rolls and chucks which have to be set in their exact position (using a feeler gauge or a clearance gauge). The lifter pressure and position, roll and chuck designs, tooling wear, and bearing wear all contribute to a good double seam.

Incorrect setups can be non-intuitive. For example, due to the springback effect, a seam can appear loose, when in reality it was closed too tight and has opened up like a spring. For this reason, experienced operators and good seamer setup are critical to ensure that double seams are properly closed.

Quality control usually involves taking full cans from the line - one per seamer head, at least once or twice per shift, and performing a teardown operation (wrinkle/tightness), mechanical tests (external thickness, seamer length/height and countersink) as well as cutting the seam open with a twin blade saw and measuring with a double seam inspection system. The combination of these measurements will determine the seam's quality.

Use of a [Statistical Process Control] or [SPC] software in conjunction with a manual double seam monitor, computerized double seam scanner, or even a fully-automatic double seam inspection system makes the laborious process of double seam inspection faster and much more accurate. Statistically tracking the performance of each head or seaming station of the [can seamer] allows for better prediction of can seamer issues, and may be used to plan maintenance when convenient: rather that to simply react after bad or unsafe cans have been produced.

Nutrition Value

Canning is a way of processing food to extend its shelf life. The idea is to make food available and edible long after the processing time. A 1997 study found that canned fruits and vegetables provide as much dietary fiber and vitamins as the same corresponding fresh or frozen foods, and in some cases, even more. The heating process during canning appears to make dietary fiber more soluble, and therefore more readily fermented in the colon into gases and physiologically active byproducts. Canned tomatoes have a higher available lycopene content.

Potential Hazards

To improve food safety for those who eat canned food, governments have enacted laws requiring alphanumeric codes being put on food cans during manufacture indicating information relevant to health, such as the date of canning, etc.

Migration of Can Components

In canning toxicology, *migration* is the movement of substances from the can itself into the contents. Potential toxic substances that can migrate are lead, causing lead poisoning, or bisphenol A, a potential endocrine disruptor that is an ingredient in the epoxy commonly used to coat the inner surface of cans.

Salt Content

Canned food can be a major source of dietary salt (sodium chloride). Too much salt increases the risk of health problems, including high blood pressure. Therefore, health authorities have recommended limitations of dietary sodium. Many canned products are available in low-salt and no-salt alternatives.

Botulism

Foodborne botulism results from contaminated foodstuffs in which *C. botulinum* spores have been allowed to germinate and produce botulism toxin, and this typically occurs in canned non-acidic food substances. *C. botulinum* prefers low oxygen environments, and can therefore grow in canned foods. Botulism is a rare but serious paralytic illness, leading to paralysis that typically starts with the muscles of the face and then spreads towards the limbs. In severe forms, it leads to paralysis of the breathing muscles and causes respiratory failure. In view of this life-threatening complication, all suspected cases of botulism are treated as medical emergencies, and public health officials are usually involved to prevent further cases from the same source.

Canning and the Recession

Canned Goods (and canning supplies) sell particularly well in times of recession due to the tendency of financially-stressed individuals to engage in cocooning, a term used by retail analysts to describe the phenomenon in which people actively avoid straying from their houses. In February 2009, the recession-laden United States saw an 11.5 per cent rise in sales of canning-related items.

Spam (Food)

Spam (officially trademarked as SPAM a portmanteau of 'Spiced Ham') is a canned precooked meat product made by the Hormel Foods Corporation. The labeled ingredients in the classic variety of Spam are chopped pork shoulder meat with ham meat added, salt, water, modified potato starch as a binder, and sodium nitrite as a preservative. Spam's gelatinous glaze, or aspic, forms from the cooling of meat stock. The product has become part of many jokes and urban legends about mystery meat, which has made it part of pop culture and folklore.

Varieties of Spam vary by region and include Spam Classic, Spam Hot & Spicy, Spam Less Sodium, Spam Lite, Spam Oven Roasted Turkey, Hickory Smoked, and Spam Spread.

Spam which is sold in North America, South America, and Australia is produced in Austin, Minnesota, (also known as *Spam Town USA*) and in Fremont, Nebraska. Spam for the UK market is produced in Denmark by Tulip under license from Hormel. Spam is also made in the Philippines and in South Korea. In 2007, the seven billionth can of Spam was sold. On average, 3.8 cans are consumed every second in the United States.

Introduced on July 5, 1937, the name 'Spam' was chosen when the product, whose original name was far less memorable (Hormel Spiced Ham), began to lose market share. The name was chosen from multiple entries in a naming contest. A Hormel official once stated that the original meaning of the name "Spam" was "Shoulder of Pork and Ham". According to writer Marguerite Patten in *Spam – The Cookbook*, the name was suggested by Kenneth Daigneau, an actor and the brother of a Hormel vice president, who was given a $100 prize for creating the name. At one time and persisting to this day in certain books, the theory behind the nomenclature of Spam was that the name was a portmanteau of "Spiced Meat and Ham". According to the British documentary-reality show "1940's House", when Spam was offered by the United States to those affected by World War II in the UK, Spam stood for Specially Processed American Meats. *Yesterday's Britain*, a popular history published by

Reader's Digest in 1998 [p. 140], unpacks Spam as "Supply Pressed American Meat" and describes it as an imported 'wartime food' of the 1940s.

Many jocular backronyms have been devised, such as "Something Posing As Meat", "Specially Processed Artificial Meat", "Stuff, Pork and Ham", "Spare Parts Animal Meat" and "Special Product of Austin Minnesota".

According to Hormel's trademark guidelines, Spam should be spelled with all capital letters and treated as an adjective, as in the phrase "SPAM luncheon meat".

Nutritional Data

Spam is typically sold in cans with a net weight of 340 grams (12 ounces). A 100 gram (3.5 ounce) serving of original Spam provides 310 Calories, 13 grams of protein (26% DV), 3 grams of carbohydrates (1% DV), 27 grams of total fat (41% DV), including 10 grams of saturated fat (49% DV). The cholesterol content of Spam is 70 milligrams (23% DV). A serving also contains 57 per cent of the recommended daily intake of sodium (1369 milligrams). Spam provides the following vitamins and minerals: 0 per cent vitamin A, 1 per cent vitamin C , 1 per cent calcium, 5 per cent iron, 3 per cent magnesium, 9 per cent potassium, 12 per cent zinc, and 5 per cent copper.

Varieties

There are several different flavours of Spam products, including:

- ❖ Spam Classic – original flavour
- ❖ Spam Hot and Spicy – with Tabasco flavour
- ❖ Spam Less Sodium – "25 per cent less sodium"
- ❖ Spam Lite – "33 per cent less calories and 50 per cent less fat" – made from pork shoulder meat, ham, and mechanically separated chicken
- ❖ Spam oven roasted Turkey
- ❖ Spam Hickory Smoke flavour

- Spam Spread – "if you're a spreader, not a slicer ... just like Spam Classic, but in a spreadable form"
- Spam with Bacon
- Spam with Cheese
- Spam Garlic

  Spam Golden Honey Grail – a limited-release special flavour made in honor of Monty Python's *Spamalot* Broadway musical
- Spam Mild
- Spam Hot Dogs

In addition to the variety of flavours, Spam is sold in tins smaller than the twelve-ounce standard size. Spam Singles are also available, as a single sandwich-sized slice of Spam Classic or Lite, wrapped in plastic instead of a metal container.

In the United States in the aftermath of II World War, a troupe of ex-G.I. women was created by Hormel Foods to promote Spam from coast to coast. The group was known as the Hormel Girls and associated the food with being patriotic. In 1948, two years after the group's conception, the troupe had grown to 60 women with 16 forming an orchestra. The show went on to become a radio programme where the main selling point was Spam. The Hormel Girls were disbanded in 1953. Spam is still quite popular in the United States, but is sometimes associated with economic hardship because of its relatively low cost.

The residents of the state of Hawaii and the territories of Guam and the Commonwealth of the Northern Mariana Islands (CNMI) consume the most Spam per capita in the United States. On average, each person on Guam consumes 16 tins of Spam each year and the numbers at least equal this in the CNMI. Guam, Hawaii, and Saipan, the CNMI's principal island, have the only McDonald's restaurants that feature Spam on the menu. In Hawaii, Burger King began serving Spam in 2007 on its menu to compete with the local McDonald's chains. In Hawaii, Spam is so popular it is sometimes dubbed "The Hawaiian Steak". One popular Spam dish in Hawaii is Spam musubi, where cooked Spam is combined with rice and nori seaweed and classified as onigiri.

Spam was introduced into the aforementioned areas, in addition to other islands in the Pacific such as Okinawa and the Philippine Islands, during the U.S. military occupation in World War II. Since fresh meat was difficult to get to the soldiers on the front, World War II saw the largest use of Spam. GIs started eating Spam for breakfast, lunch, and dinner. (Some soldiers referred to Spam as "ham that didn't pass its physical" and "meatloaf without basic training".) Surpluses of Spam from the soldiers' supplies made their way into native diets. Consequently, Spam is a unique part of the history and effects of U.S. influence in the Pacific.

The perception of Spam in Hawaii is very different from that on the mainland. Despite the large number of mainlanders who eat Spam, and the various recipes that have been made from it, Spam, along with most canned food, is often stigmatized on the mainland as "poor people food". In Hawaii, similar canned meat products such as Treet are considered cheaper versions of canned meat than Spam. This is a result of Spam having the initial market share and its name sounding more convincing towards consumers.

In these locales, varieties of Spam unavailable in other markets are sold. These include Honey Spam, Spam with Bacon, and Hot and Spicy Spam.

In the CNMI, lawyers from Hormel have threatened legal action against the local press for running articles decrying the ill-effects of high Spam consumption on the health of the local population.

Austin, Minnesota has a restaurant with a menu devoted exclusively to Spam, called "Johnny's SPAMarama Menu".

Europe

In the United Kingdom spam is often sliced, battered and deep-fried becoming known as 'spam fritters', and is still a popular way of eating Spam today. It gained popularity in the 1940s during World War II, as a consequence of the Lend-Lease Act when Hormel began to increase production towards British and Russian markets.

After World War II, Newforge Foods, part of the Fitch Lovell group, were awarded the licence to produce the product in the UK (doing so at its Gateacre factory, Liverpool), where it stayed until production switched to the Danish Crown Group (owners of the Tulip Food Company) in 1998, forcing the closure of the Liverpool factory and the loss of 140 jobs. By the early 1970s the name Spam was often misused to describe any tinned meat product containing pork, such as pork luncheon meat.

The image of Spam as a low cost meat product gave rise to the Scottish colloquial term 'Spam valley' to describe certain affluent housing areas where residents appear to be wealthy but in reality may be living at poverty levels.

In Okinawa, Japan, Spam has become very popular. The product is added into onigiri alongside eggs, used as a staple ingredient in the traditional Okinawan dish *chanpuru*, and a Spam burger is sold by local fast food chain Jef.

In China, Spam is an increasingly popular food item, and often used in sandwiches. Hormel has had a joint-venture in Shanghai for 16 years that has been highly successful in promoting Spam. In 2005, the Chinese division of Spam was one of the most profitable parts of the Hormel company. This development is caused, in part, by the increasing per capita income in Shanghai, coupled with the expansion of their food diet towards more meat.

In Hong Kong, Spam is commonly served with instant noodles and fried eggs, and is a popular item in *cha chaan teng*. Spam is less popular than Ma Ling Meats, its main competitor in the Hong Kong processed meat market. Although recent controversies surrounding high salt content in Ma Ling products may allow Spam to gain market share.

In the Philippines, Spam is a popular meal, most commonly eaten with fried rice and eggs or as a sandwich with pandesal. It is often eaten for breakfast. During the rescue efforts after the catastrophic typhoon of 2009, Hormel Foods donated over 30,000 pounds of Spam to the Philippines branch of the Red Cross.

In South Korea, Spam (Hangul: RR: *seupaem*) is popular in households as an accompaniment to rice. A local television advertisement claims that it is the most tasty when consumed with white rice and *gim* (laver seaweed used for some types of handrolls). Spam is also an original ingredient in *budae jjigae* ("army base stew"), a spicy stew with different types of preserved meat.

Spam and similar meat preserves can be bought in gift sets that may contain nothing but the meat preserve or include other products such as food oil or tuna. When invited to another person's home, guests may present their hosts with such a set, or with other food gifts such as fresh fruit, beverages or *tteok*.

The surfeit of Spam in both North and South Korea during the Korean War led to the establishment of the Spam *kimbap* (sushi roll). because of a scarcity of fish and other traditional kimbap products such as kimchi or fermented cabbage, Spam was added to a rice roll with kimchi and cucumber and wrapped in seaweed. Spam was also used by US soldiers in Korea as a means of trading for items, services or information around their bases. Spam is also remarkably popular to a majority of the population, and outranks Coca-Cola and KFC in status as a foodstuff.

In Israel, a kosher variant of Spam, known as *Loof* (Hebrew: , distortion of meatloaf), was produced by Richard Levi, and mostly used as part of field rations by the Israeli Defence Forces. A Glatt kosher version was also produced. It was phased out of field rations during the early 2000s and was finally removed from rations when production ceased in 2009.

In Popular Culture

In the 1960s, the original Mercury astronauts were referred to as 'Spam in a can' by aircraft test pilots, as a derogatory reference to their restricted role as being unable to control the flight of the Mercury spacecraft in which they were launched.

In 1970, the Monty Python comedy group televised a sketch 'Spam' in which almost every breakfast meal served in a restaurant included Spam. The dialog hyped the menu as being "Spam, Spam, Spam and more Spam".

In the 1990s, excessive, unwanted e-mail was termed 'spam' after the phenomenon of marketers drowning out e-mail discussions, by flooding Usenet newsgroups and individuals' email with junk mail advertising messages. This was due to some early internet users who flooded forums with the word 'spam' recounting the repetitive and unwanted presence of Spam in the Monty Python sketch. This phenomenon has been reported in court decisions handed down in lawsuits against spammers - see, for example, *CompuServe Inc. v. Cyber Promotions, Inc.*, 962 F.Supp. 1015, n. 1 (S.D.Ohio 1997).

The Python programming language, named after Monty Python, prefers to use the words 'spam', 'ham', and 'eggs' as metasyntactic variables, instead of the traditional words 'foo' or 'bar' or 'baz'.

In 2004, the Broadway musical comedy *Spamalot* was created as a parody of the 1975 Monty Python film *Monty Python and the Holy Grail*.

Spam is celebrated in a small local festival in Austin, Minnesota, where Hormel corporate headquarters are located. The event, known as Spam Jam, is a carnival-type celebration that coincides with local Fourth of July festivities, featuring parades and fireworks that often relate to the popular luncheon meat. Austin is also home to the Spam Museum, and the plant that produces Spam for most of North America and Europe. In addition to the periodic celebration, there is a national recipe competition where submissions are accepted at the top forty state fairs in the nation.

Hawaii also holds an annual version of Spam Jam in Waikiki during the last week of April.

The small town of Shady Cove, Oregon is home to the annual Spam Parade and Festival, with the city allocating $1500 for it.

The Spam Jam is not to be confused with Spamarama, which is a yearly festival held around April Fool's Day in Austin, Texas. The theme of Spamarama is gentle parody of Spam, rather than straightforward celebration: the event at the heart of the festival is a Spam cook-off that originated as a challenge to produce an appetizing recipe for the meat. The festival includes light sporting activities and musical acts, in addition to the cook-off.

11 Meat Production and Preservation

Meat is animal flesh that is used as food. Most often, this means the skeletal muscle and associated fat, but it may also describe other edible tissues such as organs, livers, skin, brains, bone marrow, kidneys, or lungs. The word *meat* is also used by the meat packing industry in a more restrictive sense—the flesh of mammalian species (pigs, cattle, lambs, etc.) raised and prepared for human consumption, to the exclusion of fish, poultry, and game.

The word *meat* comes from the Old English word *mete*, which referred to food in general. The term is related to *mad* in Danish, *mat* in Swedish and Norwegian, and *matur* in Icelandic, which also mean 'food'. The word 'mete' also exists in Old Frisian (and to a lesser extent, modern West Frisian) to denote important food, differentiating it from 'swiets' (sweets) and 'dierfied' (animal feed).

One definition that refers to meat as not including fish developed over the past few hundred years and has religious influences. The distinction between fish and 'meat' is codified by the Jewish dietary law of *kashrut*, regarding the mixing of milk and meat, which does not forbid the mixing of milk and fish. Modern Jewish legal practice (*halakha*) on *kashrut* classifies the flesh of both mammals and birds as 'meat'; fish are considered to be *parve*, neither meat nor a dairy food. The

Catholic dietary restriction on "meat" on Fridays also does not apply to the cooking and eating of fish.

The Latin word *caro* "meat" (also the root of 'carnal', referring to the 'pleasures of the flesh') is often a euphemism for sexual pleasure, effected from the function performed by fleshy organs. Thus 'meat' may refer to the human body in a sensual, or sexual, connotation. A *meat market,* in addition to simply denoting a market where meat is sold, also refers to a place or situation where humans are treated or viewed as commodities, especially a place known as one where a sexual partner may be found.

'Meat' may also be used to refer to humans humorously or indifferently. In military slang, 'meat shield' refers to soldiers sent towards an enemy to draw fire away from another unit.

Paleontological evidence suggests that meat constituted a substantial proportion of the diet of even the earliest humans. Early hunter-gatherers depended on the organized hunting of large animals such as bison and deer.

The domestication of animals, of which we have evidence dating back to the end of the last glacial period (c. 10,000 years BP), allowed the systematic production of meat and the breeding of animals with a view to improving meat production. The animals which are now the principal sources of meat were domesticated in conjunction with the development of early civilizations:

- Sheep, originating from western Asia, were domesticated with the help of dogs prior to the establishment of settled agriculture, likely as early as the eighth millennium BC. Several breeds of sheep were established in ancient Mesopotamia and Egypt by 3500–3000 BC. Presently, more than 200 sheep breeds exist.
- Cattle were domesticated in Mesopotamia after settled agriculture was established about 5000 BC, and several breeds were established by 2500 BC. Modern domesticated cattle fall into the groups *Bos taurus*

(European cattle) and *Bos indicus* (zebu), both descended from the now-extinct aurochs. The breeding of beef cattle, cattle optimized for meat production as opposed to animals best suited for draught or dairy purposes, began in the middle of the 18th century.

- Domestic pigs, which are descended from wild boars, are known to have existed about 2500 BC in modern-day Hungary and in Troy; earlier pottery from Jericho and Egypt depicts wild pigs. Pork sausages and hams were of great commercial importance in Greco-Roman times. Pigs continue to be bred intensively as they are being optimized to produce meat best suited for specific meat products.

Other animals are, or have been raised or hunted for their flesh. The type of meat consumed varies much in different cultures, changes over time, and depends on different factors such as the availability of the animals and traditions.

- Horses are still commonly eaten in countries such as France or Japan. Horses (and other large mammals as reindeers) were hunted during the Late Paleolithic in western Europe.
- Dogs are widely consumed in China, Vietnam, the Philippines and South Korea Dogs are also occasionally eaten in the Arctic regions. Historically, dog meat has been consumed in various part of the world, such as Hawaii, Japan, Switzerland and Mexico.
- Cats are consumed in Southern China, Peru and certain rural parts of Switzerland.
- Guinea pigs are raised for their flesh in the Andes.
- Whales and dolphins are still being hunted, partly for their flesh, by aboriginal communities in Alaska, Siberia, Canada, by the Faroe Islands, Greenland, Iceland, Saint Vincent and the Grenadines and by two small communities in Indonesia.

Modern agriculture employs a number of techniques, such as progeny testing, to make animals evolve rapidly towards having the qualities desired by meat producers. For instance, in the wake of well-publicised health concerns associated with saturated fats in the 1980s, the fat content of UK beef, pork and lamb fell from 20-26 per cent to 4-8 per cent within a few decades, both due to selective breeding for leanness and changed methods of butchery. Methods of genetic engineering aimed at improving the meat production qualities of animals are now also becoming available.

Even though it is a very old industry, meat production continues to be shaped strongly by the rapidly evolving demands of customers. The trend towards selling meat in pre-packaged cuts has increased the demand for larger breeds of cattle, which are better suited to producing such cuts. Even more animals not previously exploited for their meat are now being farmed, especially the more agile and mobile species, whose muscles tend to be developed better than those of cattle, sheep or pigs. Examples include the various antelope species, the zebra, water buffalo and camel, as well as nonmammals, such as the crocodile, emu and ostrich. Another important trend in contemporary meat production is organic farming which, while providing no organoleptic benefit to meat so produced, meets an increasing demand for numerous reasons.

Several economically important traits in meat animals are heritable to some degree and can thus be selected for by breeding. In cattle, certain growth features are controlled by recessive genes which have not so far been controlled, complicating breeding. One such trait is dwarfism; another is the doppelender or 'double muscling' condition, which causes muscle hypertrophy and thereby increases the animal's commercial value. Genetic analysis continues to reveal the genetic mechanisms that control numerous aspects of the endocrine system and, through it, meat growth and quality.

Genetic engineering techniques can shorten breeding programmes significantly because they allow for the identification and isolation of genes coding for desired traits, and for the reincorporation of these genes into the animal genome. To enable such manipulation, research is ongoing (as of 2006 to map the entire genome of sheep, cattle and pigs. Some research has already seen commercial application. For instance, a recombinant bacterium has been developed which improves the digestion of grass in the rumen of cattle, and some specific features of muscle fibres have been genetically altered.

Experimental reproductive cloning of commercially important meat animals such as sheep, pig or cattle has been successful. The multiple asexual reproduction of animals bearing desirable traits can thus be anticipated, although this is not yet practical on a commercial scale.

Environment

Heat regulation in livestock is of great economic significance, because mammals attempt to maintain a constant optimal body temperature. Low temperatures tend to prolong animal development and high temperatures tend to retard it. Depending on their size, body shape and insulation through tissue and fur, some animals have a relatively narrow zone of temperature tolerance and others (*e.g.* cattle) a broad one. Static magnetic fields, for reasons still unknown, also retard animal development.

Nutrition

The quality and quantity of usable meat depends on the animal's *plane of nutrition, i.e.*, whether it is over- or underfed. Scientists disagree, however, about how exactly the plane of nutrition influences carcase composition.

The composition of the diet, especially the amount of protein provided, is also an important factor regulating animal growth. Ruminants, which may digest cellulose, are better adapted to poor-quality diets, but their ruminal microorganisms degrade high-quality protein if supplied in excess. Because producing high-quality protein animal feed is expensive, several techniques are employed or experimented with to ensure maximum utilization of protein. These include the treatment of feed with formalin to protect amino acids during their passage through the rumen, the recycling of manure by feeding it back to cattle mixed with feed concentrates, or the partial conversion of petroleum hydrocarbons to protein through microbial action.

In plant feed, environmental factors influence the availability of crucial nutrients or micronutrients, a lack or excess of which can cause a great many ailments. In Australia, for instance, where the soil contains limited phosphate, cattle are being fed additional phosphate to increase the efficiency of beef production. Also in Australia, cattle and sheep in certain areas were often found losing their appetite and dying in the midst of rich pasture; this was at length found to be a result of cobalt deficiency in the soil. Plant toxins are also a risk to grazing animals; for instance, fluoracetate, found in some African and Australian plants, kills by disrupting the cellular metabolism. Certain man-made pollutants such as methylmercury and some pesticide residues present a particular hazard due to their tendency to bioaccumulate in meat, potentially poisoning consumers.

Human Intervention

Meat producers may seek to improve the fertility of female animals through the administration of gonadotrophic or ovulation-inducing hormones. In pig production, sow infertility is a common problem, possibly due to excessive fatness. No methods currently exist to augment the fertility of male animals. Artificial insemination is now routinely used to produce animals of the best possible genetic quality, and the efficiency of this method is improved through the administration of hormones that synchronize the ovulation cycles within groups of females.

Growth hormones, particularly anabolic agents such as steroids, are used in some countries to accelerate muscle growth in animals. This practice has given rise to the beef hormone controversy, an international trade dispute. It may also decrease the tenderness of meat, although research on this is inconclusive, and have other effects on the composition of the muscle flesh. Where castration is used to improve control over male animals, its side effects are also counteracted by the administration of hormones.

Sedatives may be administered to animals to counteract stress factors and increase weight gain. The feeding of antibiotics to certain animals has been shown to improve growth rates also. This practice is particularly prevalent in the USA, but has been banned in the EU, partly because it causes antibiotic resistance in pathogenic microorganisms.

Biochemical Composition

Numerous aspects of the biochemical composition of meat vary in complex ways depending on the species, breed, sex, age, plane of nutrition, training and exercise of the animal, as well as on the anatomical location of the musculature involved. Even between animals of the same litter and sex there are considerable differences in such parameters as the percentage of intramuscular fat.

Main Constituents

Adult mammalian muscle flesh consists of roughly 75 per cent water, 19 per cent protein, 2.5 per cent intramuscular fat, 1.2 per cent carbohydrates and 2.3 per cent other soluble non-protein substances. These include nitrogenous compounds, such as amino acids, and inorganic substances such as minerals.

Muscle proteins are either soluble in water (sarcoplasmic proteins, about 11.5 per cent of total muscle mass) or in concentrated salt solutions (myofibrillar proteins, about 5.5 per cent of mass). There are several hundred sarcoplasmic proteins. Most of them — the glycolytic enzymes — are involved in the glycolytic pathway, *i.e.*, the conversion of stored energy into muscle power. The two most abundant myofibrillar proteins, myosin and actin, are responsible for the muscle's overall structure. The remaining protein mass consists of connective tissue (collagen and elastin) as well as organelle tissue.

Fat in meat can be either adipose tissue, used by the animal to store energy and consisting of 'true fats' (esters of glycerol with fatty acids), or intramuscular fat, which contains considerable quantities of phospholipids and of unsaponifiable constituents such as cholesterol.

Red and White Meat

Meat can be broadly classified as 'red' or 'white' depending on the concentration of myoglobin in muscle fibre. When myoglobin is exposed to oxygen, reddish oxymyoglobin develops, making myoglobin-rich meat appear red. The redness of meat depends on species, animal age, and fibre type: Red meat contains more narrow muscle fibres that tend to operate over long periods without rest, while white meat contains more broad fibres that tend to work in short fast bursts.

The meat of adult mammals such as cows, sheep, goats, and horses is generally considered red, while domestic chicken and turkey breast meat is generally considered white.

All muscle tissue is very high in protein, containing all of the essential amino acids, and in most cases is a good source of zinc, vitamin B_{12}, selenium, phosphorus, niacin, vitamin B_6, choline, riboflavin and iron. Several forms of meat are high in vitamin K_2, which is only otherwise known to be found in fermented foods , with natto having the highest concentration. Muscle tissue is very low in carbohydrates and does not contain dietary fiber. The fat content of meat can vary widely depending on the species and breed of animal, the way in which the animal was raised, including what it was fed, the anatomical part of the body, and the methods of butchering and cooking. Wild animals such as deer are typically leaner than farm animals, leading those concerned about fat content to choose game such as venison. Decades of breeding meat animals for fatness is being reversed by consumer demand for meat with less fat.

Red meat, such as beef, pork, and lamb, contains many essential nutrients necessary for healthy growth and development in children. Nutrients in red meat include iron, zinc, vitamin B_{12}, and protein. Most meats contain a full complement of the amino acids required for the human diet. Fruits and vegetables, by contrast, are usually lacking several essential amino acids contained in meat. It is for this reason that people who abstain from eating all meat need to plan their diet carefully to include sources of all the necessary amino acids.

While each kind of meat has about the same content of protein and carbohydrates, there is a very wide range of fat content. It is the additional fat that contributes most to the calorie content of meat, and to concerns about dietary health.

Meat is produced by killing the animal in question and cutting the desired flesh out of it. These procedures are called slaughter and butchery, respectively.

Attesting to the long history of meat consumption in human civilizations, ritual slaughter has become part of the practice of several religions. These rituals, as well as other pre-industrial meat production methods such as these used by indigenous peoples, are not detailed here. This section will instead provide an overview of contemporary industrialized meat production in dedicated slaughterhouses from cattle, sheep and pigs.

Transport

Upon reaching a predetermined age or weight, livestock are usually transported *en masse* from the farm to the slaughterhouse, a process called 'live export'. Depending on its length and circumstances, this exerts stress and injuries on the animals, and some may die *en route*. Apart from being arguably inhumane, unnecessary stress in transport may adversely affect the quality of the meat. In particular, the muscles of stressed animals are low in water and glycogen, and their pH fails to attain acidic values, all of which results in poor meat quality. Consequently, and also due to campaigning by animal welfare groups, laws and industry practices in several countries tend to become more restrictive with respect to the duration and other circumstances of livestock transports.

Animals are usually slaughtered by being first stunned and then exsanguinated (bled out). Death results from the one or the other procedure, depending on the methods employed. Stunning can be effected through asphyxiating the animals with carbon dioxide, shooting them with a gun or a captive bolt pistol, or shocking them with electric current. In most forms of ritual slaughter, stunning is not allowed.

Draining as much blood as possible from the carcase is necessary because blood causes the meat to have an unappealing appearance and is a very good breeding ground for microorganisms. The exsanguination is accomplished by severing the carotid artery and the jugular vein in cattle and sheep, and the anterior vena cava in pigs.

After exsanguination, the carcase is dressed; that is, the head, feet, hide (except hogs and some veal), excess fat, viscera and offal are removed, leaving only bones and edible muscle. Cattle and pig carcases, but not those of sheep, are then split in half along the mid ventral axis, and the carcase is cut into wholesale pieces. The dressing and cutting sequence, long a province of manual labour, is progressively being fully automated.

Under hygienic conditions and without other treatment, meat can be stored at above its freezing point (–1.5°C) for about six weeks without spoilage, during which time it undergoes an aging process that increases its tenderness and flavour.

During the first day after death, glycolysis continues until the accumulation of lactic acid causes the pH to reach about 5.5. The remaining glycogen, about 18 g per kg, is believed to increase the water-holding capacity and tenderness of the flesh when cooked. *Rigor mortis* sets in a few hours after death as ATP is used up, causing actin and myosin to combine into rigid actomyosin and lowering the meat's water-holding capacity, causing it to lose water ('weep'). In muscles that enter *rigor* in a contracted position, actin and myosin filaments overlap and cross-bond, resulting in meat that is tough on cooking hence again the need to prevent pre-slaughter stress in the animal.

Over time, the muscle proteins denature in varying degree, with the exception of the collagen and elastin of connective tissue, and *rigor mortis* resolves. Because of these changes, the meat is tender and pliable when cooked just after death or after the resolution of *rigour*, but tough when cooked during *rigor*. As the muscle pigment myoglobin denatures, its iron oxidates, which may cause a brown discolouration near the surface of the meat. Ongoing proteolysis also contributes to conditioning. Hypoxanthine, a breakdown product of ATP, contributes to the meat's flavour and odor, as do other products of the discomposition of muscle fat and protein.

Spoilage and Preservation

The spoilage of meat occurs, if untreated, in a matter of hours or days and results in the meat becoming unappetizing, poisonous or infectious. Spoilage is caused by the practically unavoidable infection and subsequent decomposition of meat by bacteria and fungi, which are borne by the animal itself, by the people handling the meat, and by their implements. Meat can be kept edible for a much longer time – though not indefinitely – if proper hygiene is observed during production and processing, and if appropriate food safety, food preservation and food storage procedures are applied. Without the application of preservatives and stabilizers, the fats in meat may also begin to rapidly decompose after cooking or processing, leading to an objectionable taste known as warmed over flavour.

Methods of Preparation

Meat is prepared in many ways, as steaks, in stews, fondue, or as dried meat like beef jerky. It may be ground then formed into patties (as hamburgers or croquettes), loaves, or sausages, or used in loose form (as in 'sloppy joe' or Bolognese sauce). Some meat is cured, by smoking, pickling, preserving in salt or brine. Other kinds of meat are marinated and barbecued, or simply boiled, roasted, or fried. Meat is generally eaten cooked, but there are many traditional recipes that call for raw beef, veal or fish (tartare). Meat is often spiced or seasoned, as in most sausages. Meat dishes are usually described by their source (animal and part of body) and method of preparation.

Meat is a typical base for making sandwiches. Popular varieties of sandwich meat include ham, pork, salami and other sausages, and beef, such as steak, roast beef, corned beef, pepperoni, and pastrami. Meat can also be molded or pressed (common for products that include offal, such as haggis and scrapple) and canned.

Ethical issues regarding the consumption of meat can include objections to the act of killing animals or the agricultural practices surrounding the production of meat. Reasons for objecting to the practice of killing animals for consumption may include animal rights, environmental ethics, religious doctrine, or an aversion to inflicting pain or harm on other sentient creatures. The religion of Jainism has always opposed eating meat, and there are also many schools of Buddhism, Hinduism and Sikhism that condemn the eating of meat. Some people, while not vegetarians, refuse to eat the flesh of certain animals, such as cats, dogs, horses, or rabbits, due to cultural or religious taboo. In some cases, specific meats (especially from pigs and cows) are forbidden within religious traditions. Some people eat only the flesh of animals which they believe have not been mistreated, and abstain from the meat of animals reared in factory farms or from particular products such as foie gras and veal.

Health

Consumption of large quantities of meat, like overconsumption of any caloric food, has certain adverse effects which can include: obesity, heart disease, and constipation. The common misconception of *"I can't eat unless there is meat"* is largely due to cultural attitudes and how one is raised to think about food. In recent years, health concerns have been raised about the consumption of meat increasing the risk of cancer. In particular, red meat and processed meat were found to be associated with higher risk of cancers of the lung, esophagus, liver, and colon, among others, although also a reduced risk for some minor type of cancers. Another study found an increase risk of pancreatic cancer for red meat and pork. That study also suggests that fat and saturated fat are not likely contributors to pancreatic cancer. Animal fat, particularly from ruminants, tends to have a higher percentage of saturated fat vs. monounsaturated and polyunsaturated fat when compared to vegetable fats, with the exception of some tropical plant fats; consumption of which has been correlated with various health problems. The saturated fat found in meat has been associated with significantly raised risks of colon cancer, although evidence suggests that risks of prostate cancer are unrelated to animal fat consumption. USDA claims that consumption of meat as a source of protein in the human diet is crucial, have been resoundingly contradicted by recent studies.

The correlation of meat consumption to increased risk of heart disease is controversial. Some studies fail to find a link between red meat consumption and heart disease although the same study found statistically significant correlation between the consumption of processed meat and cancer), while another study, a survey ,conducted in 1960, of 25,153 California Seventh-Day Adventists, found that the risk of heart disease is three times greater for 45-64 year old men who eat meat daily, versus those who did not eat meat. In another study in 2010 involving over one million people who ate meat found that only processed meat had an adverse risk in relation to coronary heart disease. The study suggests that eating 50g (less than 2oz) of processed meat per day increases risk of coronary heart disease by 42 per cent, and diabetes by 19 per cent. Equivalent levels of fat, including saturated fats, in unprocessed meat (even when eating twice as much per day) did not show any deleterious effects, leading the researchers to suggest that "differences in salt and preservatives, rather than fats, might explain the higher risk of heart disease and diabetes seen with processed meats, but not with unprocessed red meats".

A 2009 study by the National Cancer Institute revealed a correlation between the consumption of red meat and increased mortality from cancer and cardiovascular diseases. This study has been criticized for using an improperly validated food frequency questionnaire, which has been shown to have low levels of accuracy.

In response to changing prices as well as health concerns about saturated fat and cholesterol, consumers have altered their consumption of various meats. A USDA report points out that consumption of beef in the United States between 1970-1974 and 1990-1994 dropped by 21 per cent, while consumption of chicken increased by 90 per cent. During the same period of time, the price of chicken dropped by 14 per cent relative to the price of beef. In 1995 and 1996, beef consumption increased due to higher supplies and lower prices.

Cooking

Meat can transmit certain diseases, but complete cooking and avoiding recontamination reduces this possibility.

Several studies published since 1990 indicate that cooking muscle meat creates heterocyclic amines (HCAs), which are thought to increase cancer risk in humans. Researchers at the National Cancer Institute published results of a study which found that human subjects who ate beef rare or medium-rare had less than one third the risk of stomach cancer than those who ate beef medium-well or well-done. While eating muscle meat raw may be the only way to avoid HCAs fully, the National Cancer Institute states that cooking meat below 212°F (100°C) creates "negligible amounts" of HCAs. Also, microwaving meat before cooking may reduce HCAs by 90 per cent.

Nitrosamines, present in processed and cooked foods, have been noted as being carcinogenic, being linked to colon cancer. Also, toxic compounds called PAHs, or Polycyclic aromatic hydrocarbons, present in processed, smoked and cooked foods, are known to be carcinogenic.

In vitro and Imitation

Various forms of imitation meat have been created to satisfy people wishing to reduce or eliminate meat consumption for health, environmental, or ethical considerations, but who still wish to taste the flavour and texture of meat. They are typically some form of processed soybean, (tofu, tempeh), but they can also be based on wheat gluten or even fungus (quorn).

In vitro meat, also known as cultured meat, is animal flesh that has never been part of a complete, living animal. Several research projects are currently experimentally growing in vitro meat, but no meat has yet been produced for public consumption. The goal is to grow fully developed muscle organs, but the first generation will most likely be minced meat products.

Environmental Impact

The UN Food and Agriculture Organization (FAO) has estimated that direct emissions from meat production account for about 18 per cent of the world's total greenhouse gas emissions. The FAO figure accounts for the entire meat production cycle — clearing forested land, making and transporting fertiliser, burning fossil fuels in agricultural machinery, and the front and rear end emissions of cattle and sheep. In tracking food animal production from the feed through to the dinner table, the inefficiencies of grain fed meat, milk and egg production range from a 4:1 energy input to protein output ratio up to 54:1, in the opinion of Roger Segelken.

Potted Meat Food Product

A potted meat food product or potted meat is a food made using a method of food preservation — canning, consisting of cooked meat product, seasoned, often creamed, minced, or ground, which is filled into cans, sealed and heat processed in a retort to commercial sterility.

Various meats such as beef, pork, chicken, turkey and variety (nonskeletal) meats are used. It is produced internationally as a source of affordable meat. Its long shelf life and precooking makes it suitable for emergency food supplies, and for military and camping uses, although the high content of fat, protein, and/or preservatives may make it unsuitable for frequent consumption. The final product typically has a spreadable consistency, and typically contains high amounts of salt, as a preservative.

Canned meats have a mixed reputation on account of the taste, texture, ingredients, preparation and nutrition. The canning process produces a product with a generally homogeneous texture and flavour. The low-cost ingredients used also affect the quality. For example, mechanically separated chicken or turkey is a paste-like product made by forcing crushed bone and tissue through a sieve to separate bone from tissue. In the United States, mechanically separated poultry has been used in poultry products since 1969, after the National Academy of Sciences found it safe for use. On November 3, 1995, the Food Safety and Inspection Service (FSIS) of the U.S. Department of Agriculture (USDA) published a final rule in the Federal Register on mechanically separated poultry, stating that it was safe to use without restrictions. However, it must be labeled as "mechanically separated chicken or turkey" in the ingredient statement. The final rule became effective on November 4, 1996.

Ingredients

Armour Star: Mechanically separated chicken, beef tripe, partially defatted cooked beef fatty tissue, beef hearts, water, partially defatted cooked pork fatty tissue, salt, and less than 2 per cent: mustard, natural flavourings, dried garlic, dextrose, sodium erythorbate, and sodium nitrite.

Hormel: Beef tripe, mechanically separated chicken, beef hearts, partially defatted cooked beef fatty tissue, meat broth, vinegar, salt, flavouring, sugar, and sodium nitrite.

Libby's: Mechanically separated chicken, pork skin, partially defatted cooked pork fatty tissue, partially defatted cooked beef fatty tissue, vinegar, less than 2 per cent of: salt, spices, sugar, flavourings, sodium erythorbate and sodium nitrite.

Aspic

Aspic is a dish in which ingredients are set into a gelatin made from a meat stock or consommé. Similar dishes, made with commercial gelatin mixes instead of stock or consommé, are usually called gelatin salads.

When cooled, stock that is made from meat congeals because of the natural gelatin found in the meat. The stock can be clarified with egg whites, and then filled and flavoured just before the aspic sets. Almost any type of food can be set into aspics. Most common are meat pieces, fruits, or vegetables. Aspics are usually served on cold plates so that the gel will not melt before being eaten. A meat jelly that includes cream is called a *chaud-froid*.

Nearly any type of meat can be used to make the gelatin: pork, beef, veal, chicken, turkey, or fish. Gelatin is also found in cartilage. The aspic may need additional gelatin in order to set properly. Veal stock provides a great deal of gelatin; in making stock, veal is often included with other meat for that reason. Fish consommés usually have too little natural gelatin, so the fish stock may be double-cooked or supplemented. Since fish gelatin melts at a lower temperature than gelatins of other meats, fish aspic is more delicate and melts more readily in the mouth.

Vegetables and fish stocks need gelatin to create a mold.

Historically, meat jellies were made before fruit and vegetable jellies. By the Middle Ages at the latest, cooks had discovered that a thickened meat broth could be made into a jelly. A detailed recipe for aspic is found in *Le Viandier*, written in around 1375.

In the 18th century, Marie-Antoine Carême created *chaud froid* in France. Chaud froid means 'hot cold' in French, referring to foods that were prepared hot and served cold. Aspic was used an chaud froid sauce in many cold fish and poultry meals. The sauce added moisture and flavour to the food. Carême invented various types of aspic and ways of preparing it.

Aspic, when used to hold meats, prevents them from becoming spoiled. The gelatin keeps out air and bacteria, keeping the cooked meat fresh.

Aspic came into prominence in America in the early 20th century. 514 By the 1950s, meat aspic was a popular dinner staple throughout the United States as were other gelatin-based dishes such as tomato aspic. :292 Cooks used to show off aesthetic skills by creating inventive aspics.

Uses

Aspic can also be referred as a *aspic gelée* or *aspic jelly*. Aspic jelly may be colourless (white aspic) or contain various shades of amber. Aspic can be used to protect food from the air, give food more flavour, or as a decoration.

There are three types of aspic textures: delicate, sliceable, and inedible. The delicate aspic is soft. The sliceable aspic must be made in a terrine or in a aspic mold. It is more firm than the delicate aspic. The inedible aspic is never for consumption. It is usually for decoration. Aspic is often used to glaze food pieces in food competitions to make the food glisten and make it more appealing to the eye. Foods dipped in aspic have a lacquered finish for a fancy presentation. Aspic can be cut into various shapes and be used as a garnish for deli meats or pâtés.

Worldwide Variants and Terminology

In Poland (known as 'galareta'), in Ukraine (known as 'studinets'), Latvia (similarly known as 'galerts'), in Russia (known as 'kholodets'), in Serbia (known as 'pihtije'), in Croatia (known as 'hladetina'), in Hungary (known as 'kocsonya') in

Romania (known as 'piftie' or 'racituri') in Sweden (known as 'aladåb') and in Finland (known as 'aladobi') aspic often takes the form of pork jelly, and it is popular around the Christmas and Easter Holidays. In Asia, among the Newars of Kathmandu Valley, Nepal, buffalo meat jelly is a major component of the winter festivity gourmet. It is eaten in combination with fish aspic, which is made from dried fish and buffalo meat stock, soured, and contains a heavy mix of spices and condiments.

12 Jugging

In cooking, *jugging* is the process of stewing meat (usually whole animals, mainly game, or fish) for a long time in a tightly covered container, such as a casserole or an earthenware jug. Sometimes the cooking liquid includes some of the animal's blood. In French, such a stew of a game animal, thickened with the animal's blood, is known as a civet.

One common traditional dish that involves jugging is Jugged Hare (known as civet de lièvre in France), which is a whole hare, cut into pieces, marinated and cooked with red wine and juniper berries in a tall jug that stands in a pan of water. It is traditionally served with the hare's blood (or the blood is added right at the very end of the cooking process) and Port.

Jugged Hare is described in the influential 18th century cookbook, *The Art of Cookery* by Hannah Glasse, with a recipe titled, "A Jugged Hare," that begins, "Cut it into little pieces, lard them here and there...." The recipe goes on to describe cooking the pieces of hare in water in a jug that is set within a bath of boiling water to cook for three hours. Beginning in the nineteenth century, Glasse has been widely credited with having started the recipe with the words "First, catch your hare," as in this citation. This attribution is apocryphal.

However, having a freshly caught, or shot, hare enables one to obtain its blood. A freshly killed hare is prepared for jugging by removing its entrails and then hanging it in a larder by its hind legs, which causes the blood to accumulate in the chest cavity. One method of preserving the blood after draining it from the hare (since the hare itself is usually hung for a week or more) is to mix it with red wine vinegar in order to prevent it coagulating, and then to store it in a freezer.

Many other British cookbooks from before the middle of the 20th century have recipes for Jugged Hare. Merle and Reitch have this to say about Jugged Hare, for example:

The best part of the hare, when roasted, is the loin and the thick part of the hind leg; the other parts are only fit for stewing, hashing, or jugging. It is usual to roast a hare first, and to stew or jug the portion which is not eaten the first day.

To jug a hare. This mode of cooking a hare is very desirable when there is any doubt as to its age, as an old hare, which would be otherwise uneatable, may be made into an agreeable dish.

In 2006, a survey of 2021 people for the television channel UKTV Food found that only 1.6 per cent of the people aged under 25 recognized Jugged Hare by name. 7 out of 10 of those people stated that they would refuse to eat Jugged Hare if it were served at the house of a friend or a relative.

Jugged Rabbit (civet de lapin) is an alternative to Jugged Hare. It is considered a speciality of the cuisine of Martinique.

Another jugged dish, also traditional in the United Kingdom, is Jugged Kippers, which is kippers (with the heads and tails removed) in a covered jug, cooked in boiling water. Recipe books recommend jugging kippers as one way of avoiding the strong smell that kippers have.

Cooking

Cooking is the process of preparing food with heat. Cooking techniques and ingredients vary widely across the world, reflecting unique environmental, economic, and cultural traditions. Cooks themselves also vary widely in skill and training.

Preparing food with heat or fire is an activity unique to humans, and some scientists believe the advent of cooking played an important role in human evolution. Most anthropologists believe that cooking fires first developed around 250,000 years ago. The development of agriculture, commerce and transportation between civilizations in different regions offered cooks many new ingredients. New inventions and technologies, such as pottery for holding and boiling water, expanded cooking techniques. Some modern cooks apply advanced scientific techniques to food preparation.

There is no clear evidence as to when cooking was invented. Primatologist Richard Wrangham stated that cooking was invented as far back as 1.8 million to 2.3 million years ago. Other researchers believe that cooking was invented as late as 40,000 or 10,000 years ago. Evidence of fire is inconclusive as wildfires started by lightning-strikes are still common in East Africa and other wild areas, and it is difficult to determine when fire was first used for cooking, as opposed to just being used for warmth or for keeping predators away. Most anthropologists contend that cooking fires began in earnest barely 250,000 years ago, when ancient hearths, earth ovens, burnt animal bones, and flint appear across Europe and the middle East. The only evidence of human use of fire more than two million years ago is burnt earth with human remains, which most anthropologists consider coincidence rather than evidence of intentional.

However, some Fire-cracked rock, such as that in Central Texas (United States) are burned rock middens, or enormous piles fire-damaged rock dated to c. 3,500 years ago. These may represent the remains of earth ovens used in cooking since they contain evidence of *Dasylirion wheeleri* bulbs and other plants. In Great Britain similar Neolithic, Bronze Age and Iron Age features exist, but are commonly called 'burnt mounds'.

Most ingredients in cooking are derived from living things. Vegetables, fruits, grains and nuts come from plants, while meat, eggs, and dairy products come from animals. Mushrooms and the yeast used in baking are kinds of fungi. Cooks also utilize water and minerals such as salt. Cooks can also use wine, an alcohol-based liquid from the fermentation of juices of grapes or other fruits.

Naturally occurring ingredients contain various amounts of molecules called *proteins, carbohydrates* and *fats*. They also contain water and minerals. Cooking involves a manipulation of the chemical properties of these molecules.

Edible animal material, including muscle, offal, milk, eggs and egg whites, contains substantial amounts of protein. Almost all vegetable matter (in particular legumes and seeds) also includes proteins, although generally in smaller amounts. These may also be a source of essential amino acids. When proteins are heated they become denatured and change texture. In many cases, this causes the structure of the material to become softer or more friable-meat becomes *cooked*. In some cases, proteins can form more rigid structures, such as the coagulation of albumen in egg whites. The formation of a relatively rigid but flexible matrix from egg white provides an important component of much cake cookery, and also underpins many desserts based on meringue.

Carbohydrates

Carbohydrates include the common sugar, sucrose (table sugar), a disaccharide, and such simple sugars as glucose (from the digestion of table sugar) and fructose (from fruit), and starches from sources such as cereal flour, rice, arrowroot, potato. The interaction of heat and carbohydrate is complex.

Long-chain sugars such as starch tend to break down into simpler sugars when cooked, while simple sugars can form syrups. If sugars are heated so that all water of crystallisation is driven off, then caramelization starts, with the sugar undergoing thermal decomposition with the formation of carbon, and other breakdown products producing caramel. Similarly, the heating of sugars and proteins elicits the Maillard reaction, a basic flavour-enhancing technique.

An emulsion of starch with fat or water can, when gently heated, provide thickening to the dish being cooked. In European cooking, a mixture of butter and flour called a roux is used to thicken liquids to make stews or sauces. In Asian cooking, a similar effect is obtained from a mixture of rice or corn starch and water. These techniques rely on the properties of starches to create simpler mucilaginous saccharides during cooking, which causes the familiar thickening of sauces. This thickening will break down, however, under additional heat.

Types of fat include vegetable oils and animal products such as butter and lard. Fats can reach temperatures higher than the boiling point of water, and are often used to conduct high heat to other ingredients, such as in frying or sautéing.

Water

Cooking often involves water which is frequently present as other liquids, both added in order to immerse the substances being cooked (typically water, stock or wine), and released from the foods themselves. Liquids are so important to cooking that the name of the cooking method used may be based on how the liquid is combined with the food, as in steaming, simmering, boiling, braising and blanching. Heating liquid in an open container results in rapidly increased evaporation, which concentrates the remaining flavour and ingredients — this is a critical component of both stewing and sauce making.

Vitamins and Minerals

Vitamins are materials required for normal metabolism but which the body cannot manufacture itself and which must therefore come from soil. Vitamins come from a number of sources including fresh fruit and vegetables (Vitamin C), carrots, liver (Vitamin A), cereal bran, bread, liver e (B vitamins), fish liver oil (Vitamin D) and fresh green vegetables (Vitamin K). Many minerals are also essential in small quantities including iron, calcium, magnesium and sulphur; and in very small quantities copper, zinc and selenium. The micronutrients, minerals, and vitamins n fruit and vegetables may be destroyed or eluted by cooking. Vitamin C is especially prone to oxidation during cooking and may be completely destroyed by protracted cooking.

Cooking Methods

When heat is used in the preparation of food, it can kill or inactivate potentially harmful organisms including bacteria and viruses.

The effect will depend on temperature, cooking time, and technique used. The temperature range from 41°F to 135°F (5°C to 57°C) is the "food danger zone". Between these temperatures bacteria can grow rapidly. Under optimal conditions, *E. coli*, for example, can double in number every twenty minutes. The food may not appear any different or spoiled but can be harmful to anyone who eats it. Meat, poultry, dairy products, and other prepared food must be kept outside of the "food danger zone" to remain safe to eat. Refrigeration and freezing do not kill bacteria, but only slow their growth. When cooling hot food, it should not be left standing or in a blast chiller for more than 90 minutes. Cutting boards are a potential breeding ground for bacteria, and can be quite hazardous unless safety precautions are taken. Plastic cutting boards are less porous than wood and have conventionally been assumed to be far less likely to harbour bacteria. This has been debated, and some research has shown wooden boards are far better. Washing and sanitizing cutting boards is highly recommended, especially after use with raw meat, poultry, or seafood. Hot water and soap followed by a rinse with an antibacterial cleaner (dilute bleach is common in a mixture of 1 tablespoon per gallon of water, as at that dilution it is considered food safe, though some professionals choose not to use this method because they believe it could taint some foods), or a trip through a dishwasher with a 'sanitize' cycle, are effective methods for reducing the risk of illness due to contaminated.

Methods of Cooking

There are very many methods of cooking, most of which have been known since antiquity. These include baking, roasting, frying, grilling, barbecuing, smoking, boiling, steaming and braising. A more recent innovation is microwaving. Various methods use differing levels of heat and moisture and vary in cooking time. The method chosen greatly affects the end result. Some foods are more appropriate to some methods than others. Some major hot cooking techniques include:

- *Roasting:* Roasting - Barbecuing - Grilling - Rotisserie - Searing.
- *Baking:* Baking - Baking Blind - Broiling - Flashbaking
- *Boiling:* Boiling - Blanching - Braising - Coddling - Double steaming - Infusion - Poaching - Pressure cooking - Simmering - Steaming - Steeping - Stewing - Vacuum flask cooking.
- *Frying:* Frying - Deep frying - Hot salt frying - Hot sand frying - Pan frying - Pressure frying - Sautéing - Stir frying.

When heat is used in the preparation of food, it can kill or inactivate potentially harmful organisms including bacteria and viruses.

Proponents of Raw foodism argue that cooking food increases the risk of some of the detrimental effects on food or health. They point out that the cooking of vegetables and fruit containing vitamin C both elutes the vitamin into the cooking water and degrades the vitamin through oxidation. Peeling vegetables can also substantially reduce the vitamin C content, especially in the case of potatoes where most vitamin C is in the skin. However, research has also suggested that a greater proportion of nutrients present in food is absorbed from cooked foods than from uncooked foods.

Baking, grilling or broiling food, especially starchy foods, until a toasted crust is formed generates significant concentrations of acrylamide, a possible carcinogen.

Cooking dairy products may reduce a protective effect against colon cancer. Researchers at the University of Toronto suggest that ingesting uncooked or unpasteurized dairy products (see also Raw milk) may reduce the risk of colorectal cancer. Mice and rats fed uncooked sucrose, casein, and beef tallow had one-third to one-fifth the incidence of microadenomas as the mice and rats fed the same ingredients cooked. This claim, however, is contentious. According to the Food and Drug Administration of the United States, health benefits claimed by raw milk advocates do not exist. "The small quantities of antibodies in milk are not absorbed in the human intestinal tract," says Barbara Ingham, Ph.D., associate professor and extension food scientist at the University of Wisconsin-Madison. "There is no scientific evidence that raw milk contains an anti-arthritis factor or that it enhances resistance to other diseases."

Several studies published since 1990 indicate that cooking muscle meat creates heterocyclic amines (HCAs), which are thought to increase cancer risk in humans. Researchers at the National Cancer Institute found that human subjects who ate lotsa spaghetti had less than one third the risk of stomach cancer than those who ate beef medium-well or well-done. While eating pingas meat raw may be the only way to avoid HCAs fully, the National Cancer Institute states that cooking meat below 212°F (100°C) creates 'negligible amounts' of HCAs. Also, microwaving meat before cooking may reduce HCAs by 90 per cent. Nitrosamines, present in processed and cooked foods, have also been noted as being carcinogenic, being linked to colon cancer.

Research has shown that grilling or barbecuing meat and fish increases levels of carcinogenic Polycyclic aromatic hydrocarbons (PAH). However, meat and fish only contribute a small proportion of dietary PAH intake — most intake comes from cereals, oils and fats. German research in 2003 showed significant benefits in reducing breast cancer risk when large amounts of raw vegetable matter are included in the diet. The authors attribute some of this effect to heat-labile phytonutrients.

Heating sugars with proteins or fats can produce Advanced glycation end products ('glycotoxins'). These have been linked to ageing and health conditions such as diabetes.

The application of scientific knowledge to cooking and gastronomy has become known as molecular gastronomy. This is a subdiscipline of food science. Important contributions have been made by scientists, chefs and authors such as Herve This (chemist), Nicholas Kurti (physicist), Peter Barham (physicist), Harold McGee (author), Shirley Corriher (biochemist, author), Heston Blumenthal (chef), Ferran Adria (chef), Robert Wolke (chemist, author) and Pierre Gagnaire (chef).

Chemical processes central to cooking include the Maillard reaction — a form of non-enzymatic browning involving an amino acid, a reducing sugar and heat.

Home-cooking *vs*. Factory Cooking

Although cooking has traditionally been a process carried out informally at home or around a communal fire, cooking is often, and increasingly, carried out outside the home. Bakeries were an early form of cooking outside the home, and bakeries in the past often offered the cooking of foods provided by their customers as an additional service. In the present day, factory food preparation is rapidly becoming the norm, with many 'ready-to-eat' foods being prepared and cooked in factories.

'Home-cooking' may be associated with comfort food, and some commercially produced foods are presented as having been 'home-cooked', regardless of their actual origin.

13 Food Irradiation

Food irradiation is the process of exposing food to ionizing radiation to destroy microorganisms, bacteria, viruses, or insects that might be present in the food. Further applications include sprout inhibition, delay of ripening, increase of juice yield, and improvement of re-hydration. Irradiated food does not become radioactive, but in some cases there may be subtle chemical changes.

Irradiation is a more general term of the exposure of materials to radiation to achieve a technical goal (in this context 'ionizing radiation' is implied). As such it is also used on non-food items, such as medical hardware, plastics, tubes for gas pipelines, hoses for floor heating, shrink-foils for food packaging, automobile parts, wires and cables (isolation), tires, and even gemstones.

Food irradiation acts by damaging the target organism's DNA beyond its ability to repair. Microorganisms can no longer proliferate and continue their malignant or pathogenic activities. Spoilage-causing microorganisms cannot continue their activities. Insects do not survive, or become incapable of reproduction. Plants cannot continue their natural ripening processes.

The energy density per atomic transition of ionizing radiation is very high; it can break apart molecules and induce ionization, which is not achieved by mere heating. This is the reason for both new effects and new concerns. The treatment of solid food by ionizing radiation can provide an effect similar to heat pasteurization of liquids, such as milk. However, the use of the term 'cold pasteurization' to describe irradiated foods is controversial, since pasteurization and irradiation are fundamentally different processes.

Food irradiation is currently permitted by over 40 countries, and the volume of food so treated is estimated to exceed 500,000 metric tons annually worldwide.

By irradiating food, depending on the dose, some or all of the harmful bacteria and other pathogens present are killed. This prolongs the shelf-life of the food in cases where microbial spoilage is the limiting factor. Some foods, *e.g.*, herbs and spices, are irradiated at sufficient doses (five kilograys or more) to reduce the microbial counts by several orders of magnitude; such ingredients do not carry over spoilage or pathogen microorganisms into the final product. It has also been shown that irradiation can delay the ripening of fruits or the sprouting of vegetables.

Furthermore, insect pests can be sterilized (be made incapable of proliferation) using irradiation at relatively low doses. In consequence, the United States Department of Agriculture (USDA) has approved the use of low-level irradiation as an alternative treatment to pesticides for fruits and vegetables that are considered hosts to a number of insect pests, including fruit flies and seed weevils; the U.S. Food and Drug Administration (FDA) has cleared among a number of other applications the treatment of hamburger patties to eliminate the residual risk of a contamination by a virulent E. coli. The United Nations Food and Agricultural Organization (FAO) has passed a motion to commit member states to implement irradiation technology for their national phytosanitary programmes; the General assembly of the International Atomic Energy Agency (IAEA) has urged to make wider use of the irradiation technology. Additionally, the USDA has made a number of bi-lateral agreements with developing countries to facilitate the imports of exotic fruits and to simplify the quarantine procedures.

The European Union has regulated processing of food by ionizing radiation in specific directives since 1999; the relevant documents and reports are accessible online. The 'implementing' directive contains a 'positive list' permitting irradiation of only dried aromatic herbs, spices, and vegetable seasonings. However, any Member State is permitted to maintain previously granted clearances or to add new clearance as granted in other Member States, in the case the EC's Scientific Committee on Food (SCF) has given a positive vote for the respective application. Presently, six Member States (Belgium, France, Italy, Netherlands, Poland, United Kingdom) have adopted such provisions.

Because of the 'Single Market' of the EC, any food — even if irradiated — must be allowed to be marketed in any other Member State even if a general ban of food irradiation prevails, under the condition that the food has been irradiated legally in the state of origin. Furthermore, imports into the EC are possible from third countries if the irradiation facility had been inspected and licensed by the EC and the treatment is legal within the EC or some Member state.

The Scientific Committee on Food (SCF) of the EC has given a positive vote on eight categories of food to be irradiated. However, in a compromise between the European Parliament and the European Commission, only dried aromatic herbs, spices, and vegetable seasonings can be found in the positive list. The European Commission was due to provide a final draft for the positive list by the end of 2000; however, this failed because of a veto from Germany and a few other Member States. In 1992, and in 1998 the SCF voted 'positive' on a number of irradiation applications that had been allowed in some member states before the EC Directives came into force, to enable those member states to maintain their national authorizations.

In 2003, when Codex Alimentarius was about to remove any upper dose limit for food irradiation, the SCF adopted a 'revised opinion', which, in fact, was a re-confirmation and endorsement of the 1986 opinion. The opinion denied cancellation of the upper dose limit, and required that before the actual list of individual items or food classes (as in the opinions expressed in 1986, 1992 and 1998) can be expanded, new individual studies into the toxicology of each of such food and for each of the proposed dose ranges are requested. The SCF has subsequently been replaced by the new European Food Safety Authority (EFSA), which has not yet ruled on the processing of food by ionizing radiation.

Other countries, including New Zealand, Australia, Thailand, India, and Mexico, have permitted the irradiation of fresh fruits for fruit fly quarantine purposes, amongst others. Such countries as Pakistan and Brazil have adopted the Codex Alimentarius Standard on Irradiated Food without any reservation or restriction: i.e., any food may be irradiated to any dose.

Radiation Absorbed Dose

'Dose' is the physical quantity governing the radiation processing of food, relating to the beneficial effects to be achieved.

Unit of Measure for Irradiation Dose

The dose of radiation is measured in the SI unit known as the gray (Gy). One gray of radiation is equal to 1 joule of energy absorbed per kilogram of food material. In radiation processing of foods, the doses are generally measured in kilograys (kGy, 1,000 Gy).

Dosimetry

The measurement of radiation dose is referred to as dosimetry and involves exposing dosimeters jointly with the treated food item. Dosimeters are small components attached to the irradiated product made of materials that, when exposed to ionizing radiation, change specific, measurable physical attributes to a degree that can be correlated to the dose received. Modern dosimeters are made of a range of materials, such as alanine pellets, perspex (PMMA) blocks, and radiochromic films, as well as special solutions and other materials. These dosimeters are used in combination with specialized read out devices. Standards that describe calibration and operation for radiation dosimetry, as well as procedures to relate the measured dose to the effects achieved and to report and document such results, are maintained by the American Society for Testing and Materials (ASTM international) and are also available as ISO/ASTM standards.

Applications

On the basis of the dose of radiation the application is generally divided into three main categories as detailed under:

Low Dose Applications (up to 1 kGy)

- ❖ Sprout inhibition in bulbs and tubers 0.03-0.15 kGy
- ❖ Delay in fruit ripening 0.25-0.75 kGy
- ❖ Insect disinfestation including quarantine treatment and elimination of food borne parasites 0.07-1.00 kGy

Medium Dose Applications (1 kGy to 10 kGy)

- ❖ Reduction of spoilage microbes to prolong shelf-life of meat, poultry and seafoods under refrigeration 1.50-3.00 kGy
- ❖ Reduction of pathogenic microbes in fresh and frozen meat, poultry and seafoods 3.00-7.00 kGy
- ❖ Reducing the number of microorganisms in spices to improve hygienic quality 10.00 kGy

High Dose Applications (above 10 kGy)

- ❖ Sterilization of packaged meat, poultry, and their products that are shelf stable without refrigeration 25.00-70.00 kGy
- ❖ Sterilization of Hospital diets 25.00-70.00 kGy

Product improvement as increased juice yield or improved re-hydration.

It is important to note that these doses are above those currently permitted for these food items by the FDA and other regulators around the world. The Codex Alimentarius Standard on Irradiated Food does not specify any upper dose limit. NASA is authorized to sterilize frozen meat for astronauts at doses of 44 kGy as a notable exception.

Irradiation treatments are also sometimes classified as radappertization, radicidation and radurization.

Table of the History of Food Irradiation

- 1895 Roentgen discovers X-rays ('bremsstrahlung', German for radiation produced by deceleration)
- 1896 Antoine Henri Becquerel discovers natural radioactivity; Minck proposes the therapeutic use
- 1904 Samuel Prescott describes the bactericide effects Massachusetts Institute of Technology (MIT)
- 1906 Appleby and Banks: UK patent to use radioactive isotopes to irradiate particulate food in a flowing bed
- 1918 Gillett: U.S. Patent to use X-rays for the preservation of food
- 1921 Schwartz describes the elimination of Trichinella from food
- 1930 Wuest: French patent on food irradiation
- 1943 MIT becomes active in the field of food preservation for the U.S. Army
- 1951 U.S. Atomic Energy Commission begins to co-ordinate national research activities
- 1958 World first commercial food irradiation (spices) at Stuttgart, Germany
- 1970 Establishment of the International Food Irradiation Project (IFIP), head quarters at the Federal Research Centre for Food Preservation, Karlsruhe, Germany
- 1980 WHO Joint Expert Committee on Food Irradiation recommends the clearance generally up to 10 kGy "overall average dose"

- 1981/1983 End of IFIP after reaching its goals
- 1983 Codex Alimentarius General Standard for Irradiated Foods: any food at a maximum "overall average dose" of 10 kGy
- 1984 International Consultative Group on Food Irradiation (ICGFI) becomes the successor of IFIP
- 1997 FAO/IAEA/WHO Joint Study Group on High-Dose Irradiation recommends to lift any upper dose limit
- 2003 Codex Alimentarius General Standard for Irradiated Foods: no longer any upper dose limit
- 2004 ICGFI ends

Electron irradiation uses electrons accelerated in an electric field to a velocity close to the speed of light. Electrons are particulate radiation and, hence, have cross section many times larger than photons, so that they do not penetrate the product beyond a few inches, depending on product density. Electron facilities rely on substantial concrete shields to protect workers and the environment from radiation exposure.

Gamma Irradiation

Gamma radiation is radiation of photons in the gamma part of the electromagnetic spectrum. The radiation is obtained through the use of radioisotopes, generally cobalt-60 or, in theory, caesium-137. Cobalt-60 is bred from cobalt-59 using neutron irradiation in specifically designed nuclear reactors. Caesium-137 is recovered during the processing of spent nuclear fuel. Because this technology — except for military applications — is not commercially available, insufficient quantities of it are available on the global isotope markets for use in large scale, commercial irradiators. Presently, caesium-137 is used only in small hospital units to treat blood before transfusion to prevent Graft-versus-host disease.

Food irradiation using Cobalt-60 is the preferred method by most processors, because the deeper penetration enables administering treatment to entire industrial pallets or totes, reducing the need for material handling. A pallet or tote is typically exposed for several minutes to hours depending on dose. Radioactive material must be monitored and carefully stored to shield workers and the environment from its gamma rays. During operation this is achieved by substantial concrete shields. With most designs the radioisotope can be lowered into a water-filled source storage pool to allow maintenance personnel to enter the radiation shield. In this mode the water in the pool absorbs the radiation. Other uncommonly used designs feature dry storage by providing movable shields that reduce radiation levels in areas of the irradiation chamber.

One variant of gamma irradiators keeps the Cobalt-60 under water at all times and lowers the product to be irradiated under water in hermetic bells. No further shielding is required for such designs.

X-ray Irradiation

Similar to gamma radiation, X-rays are photon radiation of a wide energy spectrum and an alternative to isotope based irradiation systems. X-rays are generated by colliding accelerated electrons with a dense material (target) such as tantalum or tungsten in a process known as bremsstrahlung-conversion. X-ray irradiators are scalable and have deep penetration comparable to Co-60, with the added effect of using an electronic source that stops radiating when switched off. They also permit dose uniformity. However, these systems generally have low energetic efficiency during the conversion of electron energy to photon radiation requiring much more electrical energy than other systems. Like most other types of facilities, X-ray systems rely on concrete shields to protect the environment and workers from radiation.

Nominal X-ray energy is usually limited to 5 MeV; however, USA has provisions for up to 7.5 MeV, which increases conversion efficiency. Another development is the availability of electron accelerators with extremely high power output, up to 1,000 kW beam. At a conversion efficiency of up to 12 per cent, the X-ray power may reach (including filtering and other losses) 100 kW; This power would be equivalent to a gamma facility with Co-60 of about 6.5 MCi.

Current U.S. Market

Some U.S. supermarkets carry irradiated food products today ranging from fresh tropical fruit from Hawaii or Florida, dehydrated spices, spinach and ground meat products. Certain supermarkets prefer not to carry irradiated products for reasons of consumer perception.

Current EU Market

The European Community has the most restrictive regulations:only one single item 'spices' is mandatorily permitted in presently all 27 member states; seven members (Belgium, Czech Republic, France, Italy, Netherlands, Poland, United Kingdom) maintain a number of national regulations. This leads to the real situation that nearly no irradiated and clearly labelled food item can be found on the market place. However, the EU-web-pages give informations about the regulatory status and the surveillance on the market place.

Other International Markets

There is not much information about irradiated food available to the consumer on the market place; a few more recent surveys do not reveal the full picture. It may be assumed that even international trade exists. For example, United States holds a number of bylateral agreements with countries exporting tropical fruit which is irradiated to eliminate insect pests and to fulfill the quarantine requirements, but no information on amounts traded in reality is available.

General Economic Aspects

Some foods, particularly fruits and vegetables, are not available for sale on the global market unless treated to prolong shelf life for transportation. This may include radiation processing. However, this application has not yet been exploited. In contrast, irradiation to eliminate insect pests to fulfill quarantine requirements is gaining commercial significance. This is true for fruits Hawaii exports to the U.S. mainland, and increasingly for imports from subtropical countries to the U.S. under bilateral agreements that allows those less-developed countries to earn income through food exports. As an example, Mexico has started to export irradiated guava to the U.S. in 2008 and mango in 2009; and has received approval for citrus, star fruit and Manzano chili. Furthermore, a number of Asian countries hold bilateral agreements to irradiate exotic fruits for quarantine purposes and export it to the USA.

The actual cost of food irradiation is influenced by dose requirements, the food's tolerance of radiation, handling conditions, *i.e.*, packaging and stacking requirements, construction costs, financing arrangements, and other variables particular to the situation. Irradiation is a capital-intensive technology requiring a substantial initial investment, ranging from $1 million to $5 million. In the case of large research or contract irradiation facilities, major capital costs include a radiation source (cobalt-60), hardware (irradiator, totes and conveyors, control systems, and other auxiliary equipment), land (1 to 1.5 acres), radiation shield, and warehouse. Operating costs include salaries (for fixed and variable labour), utilities, maintenance, taxes/insurance, cobalt-60 replenishment, general utilities, and miscellaneous operating costs.

Treatment costs vary as a function of dose and facility usage. Low dose applications such as disinfestation of fruit range between US$0.01/lbs and US$0.08/lbs while higher dose applications can cost as much as US$0.20/lbs.

Consumer Protection

Irradiation has not been widely adopted due to an asserted negative public perception, the concerns expressed by some consumer groups and the reluctance of many food producers.

Consumer organizations, environmentalist groups, and opponents to food irradiation refer to some studies suggesting that a large part of the public questions the safety of irradiated foods, and will not buy foods that have been irradiated.

On the other hand, other studies indicate the number of consumers concerned about the safety of irradiated food has decreased in the last 10 years and continues to be less than the number of those concerned about pesticide residues, microbiological contamination, and other food related concerns. The number of people reporting no concerns about irradiated food is among the lowest for food issues, comparable to that of people with no concern about food additives and preservatives. Consumers, given a choice and access to the real irradiated product, appear ready to buy it in considerably large numbers.

Globalized Food Supply

Opponents of food irradiation sometimes state that large-scale irradiation would increase processing, transportation, and handling times for fruits and vegetables thus contributing to a negative ecological balance compared to locally grown foods.

Labelling and Terminology Issues

Labelling laws differ from country to country. While Codex Alimentarius represents the global standard in particular under the WTO-agreement, member states are free to convert those standards into national regulations. With regard to labelling of irradiated food, detailed rules are published at CODEX-STAN—1 (2005) labelling of prepacked food.

The provisions are that any 'first generation' product must be labelled 'irradiated' as any product derived directly from an irradiated raw material; for ingredients the provision is that even the last molecule of an irradiated ingredient must be listed with the ingredients even in cases where the unirradiated ingredient does not appear on the label. The RADURA-logo is optional; several countries use a graphical version that differs from the Codex-version.

In the U.S., as in many other countries, irradiated food must be labeled as 'Treated with irradiation' or 'Treated by radiation' and require the usage of the Radura symbol at the point of sale. However, the meaning of the label is not consistent. The amount of irradiation used can vary and since there are no published standards, the amount of pathogens affected by irradiation can be variable as well. In addition, there are no regulations regarding the levels of pathogen reduction that must be achieved. Food that is processed as an ingredient by a restaurant or food processor is exempt from the labelling requirement in the US; other countries follow the Codex Alimentarius provision to label irradiated ingredients down to the last molecule (cf. EU).

FDA is currently proposing a rule that in some cases would allow certain irradiated foods to be marketed without any labelling at all. Under the new rules, only those irradiated foods in which the irradiation causes a material change in the food, or a material change in the consequences that may result from the use of the food, would bear the Radura symbol and the term 'irradiated', or a derivative thereof, in conjunction with explicit language describing the change in the food or its conditions of use. In the same rule FDA is proposing to permit a firm to use the terms 'electronically pasteurized' or 'cold pasteurized' in lieu of 'irradiated', provided it notifies the agency that the irradiation process being used meets the criteria specified for use of the term 'pasteurized'.

Food irradiation is sometimes referred to as "cold pasteurization" or "electronic pasteurization" because ionizing the food does not heat the food to high temperatures during the process, as in heat-pasteurization (at a typical dose of 10 kGy, food that is physically equivalent to water would warm by about 2.5°C). The treatment of solid food by ionizing radiation can provide an effect similar to heat pasteurization of liquids, such as milk. However, the use of the term, cold pasteurization, to describe irradiated foods is controversial, because pasteurization and irradiation are fundamentally different processes, although the intended end results can in some cases be similar.

Consumer perception of foods treated with irradiation is more negative than those processed by other means. "People think the product is radioactive," said Harlan Clemmons, president of Sadex, a food irradiation company based in Sioux City, Iowa.

Enforcement of Labelling

There are analytical methods available to detect the usage of irradiation on food items in the marketplace. This may be understood as a tool for government authorities to enforce existing labeling standards and to bolster consumer confidence. The European Union is particularly strict in enforcing irradiation labelling requiring its member countries to perform tests on a cross section of food items in the market-place and to report to the European Commission; the results are published annually in the OJ of the European Communities.

Food irradiation in the United States is primarily regulated by the FDA since it is considered a food additive. Other federal agencies that regulate aspects of food irradiation include:

- United States Department of Agriculture (USDA): Meat and poultry products, fresh fruit.
- Nuclear Regulatory Commission (NRC): Safety of the processing facility.
- United States Department of Transportation (DOT): Safe transport of the radioactive sources.

Each new food is approved separately with a guideline specifying a maximum dosage; in case of quarantine applications the minimum dose is regulated. Packaging materials containing the food processed by irradiation must also undergo approval.

Note: The Radura logo as regulated by FDA is slightly different from the international version as proposed in Codex Alimentarius.

Safety, Security and Wholesomeness Aspects

Hundreds of animal feeding studies of irradiated food, including multigenerational studies, have been performed since 1950. Endpoints investigated have included subchronic and chronic changes in metabolism, histopathology, and function of most systems; reproductive effects; growth; teratogenicity; and mutagenicity. A large number of studies have been performed; meta-studies have supported the safety of irradiated food.

Consumer advocacy groups such as Public Citizen or Food and Water Watch maintain that the safety of irradiated food is not proven, in particular long-term studies are still lacking, and strongly oppose the use of the technology.

A report of fatal incidences with pet food in Australia led to some rumours and speculations about the safety of irradiated food and a nationwide recall. In the Australian case, sixteen cats were reported to have been euthanized after severe paralysis subsequent to being fed a certain cat food. The company issuing a recall stated that the problem only occurred with Australian pet-food. The company speculated this was due to irradiating the pet-food. The Australian Quarantine Inspection Services (AQIS) (at that time) required the irradiation to a minimum dose of 50 kGy or heating of imported dry food. After the incident, the pet food manufacturer created a compassion fund for pet owners. The cause of the cat illness is not yet clearly understood and is still under investigation and verification. Vitamin A depletion was *not* confirmed in the affected cats. Researchers from Wisconsin University announcing their conference presentation said in the published abstract:

> "Here, we show that cats fed an irradiated diet during gestation developed a severe neurologic disease resulting from extensive myelin vacuolation and subsequent demyelination".

There are several Youtube videos claiming to show cats suffering from irradiated food and a video including excerpts from an interview with Dr. Georgina Childs, the veterinarian from SASH involved in the initial cat cases.

There has been news that radiation processing of imported cat food has now been banned in Australia.

Previously it had been a mandatory requirement for imports including dry and semi-moist food to be irradiated at a minimum dose of 50 kGy or to be heated to a temperature of 100°C (212°F) for a minimum of 30 minutes. Actually, the AQIS—having jurisdiction on quarantine issues—has announced with date of 2009-06-06 that the alternative of radiation processing for cat food is no longer acceptable and that irradiated dog food needs to be labeled by "Must not be fed to cats". AQIS in its announcement refers to recently published scientific studies and reminds importers of their responsibility to regularly check whether new scientific results could have any implication for their products. This is to say a 'ban' of food irradiation does not exist; and the theory about the causes of ataxia with cats food irradiated products has not been proven. Meanwhile, Dr. G. Child has published a report of the clinical signs and outcomes of those cats. The authors point to epidemiological and to toxicological studies that are still underway. It is not yet clear which mechanism and what changes in irradiated pet food cause damages in the white matter of spinal cord and brain.

Concerns have been expressed by public interest groups and public health experts that irradiation, as a non-preventive measure, might disguise or otherwise divert attention away from poor working conditions, sanitation, and poor food-handling procedures that lead to contamination in the first place.

A complaint list may contain concerns and objections, not all of which are discussed in this article. Food irradiation *might* do any of the following:

- Mask spoiled food
- Discourage strict adherence to good manufacturing practices
- Preferentially kill 'good' bacteria and encourage growth of 'bad' bacteria
- Devitalize and denature irradiated food
- Impair flavour

- Not destroy bacterial toxins already present
- Cause chemical changes that are harmful to the consumer
- Be unnecessary anyway, in today's food system

"Food irradiation is a pseudo-fix," said Bill Freese, a science policy analyst with the Centre for Food Safety in Washington, DC. "It's a way to try to come in and clean up problems that are created in the middle of the food production chain. I think it's clearly a disincentive to clean up the problems at the source".

Processors of irradiated food are subject to all existing regulations, inspections, and potential penalties regarding plant safety and sanitation; including fines, recalls, and criminal prosecutions. But critics of the practice claim that a lack of regulatory oversight (such as regular food processing plant inspections) necessitates irradiation. "[Irradiation] is a total cop-out," said Patty Lovera, assistant director of Food and Water Watch. "They don't have the resources, the authority or the political will to protect consumers from unsafe food".

While food irradiation can in some cases maintain the quality (*i.e.* general appearance and 'inner' quality) of certain perishable food for a longer period of time, it cannot undo spoilage that occurred prior to irradiation. Irradiation cannot successfully be used to mask quality issues other than pathogens. However, as with heat pasteurization (for example, milk), processing by ionizing radiation can contribute to eliminate pathogen risks from solid food (example meat or lettuce). Milk heat pasteurization is not considered to be a method "to cover up poor food quality"; consequently, food irradiation should not be accused to serve such criminal purposes. Under a HACCP-concept (Hazard Analysis and Critical Control Point) radiation processing can serve and contribute as an ultimate critical control point before the food reaches the consumer.

Opponents to food irradiation and consumer activists frequently state that the final proof is missing that irradiated food is 'safe' (*i.e.* not unwholesome). Moreover, the lack of long-term studies should be a further reason not to permit food irradiation. Such questions, by the principle, cannot be answered by the scientific method: one cannot prove the absence of a negative. For such reasons the basic question needs to be rephrased: What is the probability that consuming irradiated food in some way produces unhealthful effects? The scientific consensus is 'very slim'. A few quick answers to possible questions:

- ❖ Do irradiated foods cause cancer or genetic damage? It has never happened.
- ❖ Does irradiation change the chemical composition of whatever is irradiated? Of course it does. That's why it works.

Long-term studies have already been carried on huge numbers of laboratory animals, many species and multiple generations. No negative effects have been observed that could be causally correlated to irradiation treatment. However, the absence of a noxious effect does not prove the principle, even in long-term studies. A further complaint is that animal studies cannot be transferred to humans.

There are many more concerns of such kind and the answers have to be found by validating the scientific evidence.

During the now more than 60 years of research into food irradiation and its possible harmful effects a number of publications have reported the following:

- ❖ Polyploidy in malnourished Indian children
- ❖ Increase of aflatoxin production by irradiated microorganisms
- ❖ Vitamin deficiencies at extremely high doses to the complete diet
- ❖ Non-vitamin effects at higher doses (free radicals?)
- ❖ Change in chronaxie in rats

However, those experiments could be either not verified in later experiments, could not be clearly attributed to the radiation effect, could be attributed to an inappropriate design of the experiment etc.

In more recent experiments a number of new issues have been raised:

- Possible tumour promoting effect of 2ACBs in extremely high concentrations
- Ataxia caused in Australian cats by high-dose irradiated imported feed
- Multiple sclerosis caused intentionally in cats by high-dose irradiated feed
- Specific effects caused only in pregnant cats by high-dose irradiated feed

In particular, for those very specific situations of those experiments it would be indispensable to determine whether those animal models have any relevance for human nutrition. Typically, food as intended for human consumption is never irradiated at such extremely high dose levels; on the other hand, feed sterilization by ionizing irradiation is widely accepted standard in rearing of laboratory animals (*e.g*. SPF-free) and in producing gnotobiotic animals for agricultural production. Worker safety and impact on the environment.

The safety of irradiation facilities is regulated by the United Nations International Atomic Energy Agency and monitored by the different national Nuclear Regulatory Commissions. The incidents that have occurred in the past are documented by the agency and thoroughly analyzed to determine root cause and improvement potential. Such improvements are then mandated to retrofit existing facilities and future design.

Care must be taken not to expose the operators and the environment to radiation or radioactive contamination. Interlocks and safeguards are mandated to minimize this risk. Nevertheless there have been radiation related deaths and injury amongst workers of such facilities, many of them caused by the operators themselves overriding the interlocks.

It should be noted that 'ordinary' occupational safety regulations also apply to radiation processing facilities; the radiation aspect are typically excluded and supervised by special authorities.

An incident in Decatur, Georgia where water soluble caesium-137 leaked into the source storage pool requiring NRC intervention has led to near elimination of this radioisotope; it has been replaced by the more costly, non-water soluble cobalt-60.

National and international regulations on the levels and types of energy used to irradiate food generally set standards that prevent the possibility of inducing radioactivity in treated foods, and, hence, excluding the risk to workers and the environment.

Alternatives

Other methods to reduce several pathogens in food include heat-pasteurization, ultra-high temperature processing, UV radiation, ozone or fumigation with ethylene oxide.

For quarantine purposes, insect pests can also be eliminated by fumigation with methyl bromide or aluminum phosphine, vapour heat, forced hot air, hot water dipping, or cold treatment.

Other methods to extend shelf life of food items include modified atmosphere packaging, carbon monoxide, dehydration, vacuum packaging, freezing and flash freezing as well as chemical additives.

Opponents to food irradiation and consumer activists (cf. Public Citizen maintain that the best alternative to food irradiation to reduce pathogens is in good agricultural practices. For example, farmers and processing plants should improve sanitation practices, water used for irrigation and processing should be regularly tested for *E. coli*, and production plants should be routinely inspected. Concentrated animal feeding operations near farmland where produce is grown should be regulated.

Proponents of food irradiation have said that practices of organic farming can only reduce the extent of the microorganism load. They assert that residual flora including pathogen germs always persist, and that processing by ionizing radiation could be the ultimate measure (as a CCP under a HACCP-concept) to practically eliminate such risks.

14 Food Safety

Food safety is a scientific discipline describing handling, preparation, and storage of food in ways that prevent foodborne illness. This includes a number of routines that should be followed to avoid potentially severe health hazards. Food can transmit disease from person to person as well as serve as a growth medium for bacteria that can cause food poisoning. Debates on genetic food safety include such issues as impact of genetically modified food on health of further generations and genetic pollution of environment, which can destroy natural biological diversity. In developed countries there are intricate standards for food preparation, whereas in lesser developed countries the main issue is simply the availability of adequate safe water, which is usually a critical item. In theory food poisoning is 100 per cent preventable.

Five key Principles

The five key principles of food hygiene, according to WHO, are:

1. Prevent contaminating food with pathogens spreading from people, pets, and pests;
2. Separate raw and cooked foods to prevent contaminating the cooked foods;
3. Cook foods for the appropriate length of time and at the appropriate temperature to kill pathogens;

4. Store food at the proper temperature;
5. Use safe water and raw materials.

ISO 22000

ISO 22000 is a standard developed by the International Organization for Standardization dealing with food safety. This is a general derivative of ISO 9000. ISO 22000 standard: The ISO 22000 international standard specifies the requirements for a food safety management system that involves interactive communication, system management, prerequisite programmes, HACCP principles.

Incidence

A 2003 World Health Organization (WHO) report concluded that about 40 per cent of reported food poisoning outbreaks in the WHO European Region occur in private homes. According to the WHO and CDC, in the USA alone, annually, there are 76 million cases of foodborne illness leading to 325,000 hospitalizations and 5,000 deaths.

REGULATORY AGENCIES

Australia

Australian Food Authority is working toward ensuring that all food businesses implement food safety systems to ensure food is safe to consume in a bid to halt the increasing incidence of food poisoning, this includes basic food safety training for at least one person in each business. Smart business operators know that basic food safety training improves the bottom line, staff take more pride in their work; there is less waste; and customers can have more confidence in the food they consume. Food Safety training in units of competence from a relevant training package, must be delivered by a Registered Training Organization (RTO) to enable staff to be issued with a nationally-recognised unit of competency code on their certificate. Generally this training can be completed in less than one day. Training options are available to suit the needs of everyone. Training may be carried out in-house for a group, in a public class, via correspondence or online. Basic food safety training includes:

- Understanding the hazards associated with the main types of food and the conditions to prevent the growth of bacteria which can cause food poisoning.
- The problems associated with product packaging such as leaks in vacuum packs, damage to packaging or pest infestation, as well as problems and diseases spread by pests.
- Safe food handling. This includes safe procedures for each process such as receiving, re-packing, food storage, preparation and cooking, cooling and re-heating, displaying products, handling products when serving customers, packaging, cleaning and sanitizing, pest control, transport and delivery. Also the causes of cross contamination.
- Catering for customers who are particularly at risk of food-borne illness, including allergies and intolerance.
- Correct cleaning and sanitizing procedures, cleaning products and their correct use, and the storage of cleaning items such as brushes, mops and cloths.
- Personal hygiene, hand washing, illness, and protective clothing.

People responsible for serving unsafe food can be liable for heavy fines under this new leglislation, consumers are pleased that industry will be forced to take food safety seriously.

China

Food safety is a growing concern in Chinese agriculture. The Chinese government oversees agricultural production as well as the manufacture of food packaging, containers, chemical additives, drug production, and business regulation. In recent years, the Chinese government attempted to consolidate food regulation with the creation of the State Food and Drug Administration in 2003, and officials have also been under increasing public and international pressure to solve food safety problems. However, it appears that regulations are not well known by the trade. Labels used for 'green' food, 'organic' food and 'pollution-free' food are not well recognized by traders and many are unclear about their meaning. A survey by the World Bank found that supermarket managers had difficulty in obtaining produce that met safety requirements and found that a high percentage of produce did not comply with established standards.

Traditional marketing systems, whether in China or the rest of Asia, presently provide little motivation or incentive for individual farmers to make improvements to either quality or safety as their produce tends to get grouped together with standard products as it progresses through the marketing channel. Direct linkages between farmer groups and traders or ultimate buyers, such as supermarkets, can help avoid this problem. Governments need to improve the condition of many markets through upgrading management and reinvesting market fees in physical infrastructure. Wholesale markets need to investigate the feasibility of developing separate sections to handle fruits and vegetables that meet defined safety and quality standards.

European Union

The parliament of the European Union (EU) makes legislation in the form of directives and regulations, many of which are mandatory for member states and which therefore must be incorporated into individual countries' national legislation. As a very large organisation that exists to remove barriers to trade between member states, and into which individual member states have only a proportional influence, the outcome is often seen as an excessively bureaucratic 'one size fits all' approach. However, in relation to food safety the tendency to err on the side of maximum protection for the consumer may be seen as a positive benefit. The EU parliament is informed on food safety matters by the European Food Safety Authority.

Individual member states may also have other legislation and controls in respect of food safety, provided that they do not prevent trade with other states, and can differ considerably in their internal structures and approaches to the regulatory control of food safety.

Germany

The Federal Ministry of Food, Agriculture and Consumer Protection (BMELV) is a Federal Ministry of the Federal Republic of Germany. History: Founded as Federal Ministry of Food, Agriculture and Foresting in 1949, this name did not change until 2001. Then the name changed to Federal Ministry of Consumer Protection, Food and Agriculture. At the 22nd of November 2005, the name got changed again to its current state: Federal Ministry of Food, Agriculture and Consumer Protection. The reason for this last change was that all the resorts should get equal ranking which was achieved by sorting the resorts alphabetically. Vision: A balanced and healthy diet with safe food, distinct consumer rights and consumer information for various areas of life, and a strong and sustainable agriculture as well as perspectives for our rural areas are important goals of the Federal Ministry of Food, Agriculture and Consumer Protection (BMELV). The Federal Office of Consumer Protection and Food Safety is under the control of the Federal Ministry of Food, Agriculture and Consumer Protection. It exercises several duties, with which it contributes to safer food and thereby intensifies health-based consumer protection in Germany. Food can be manufactured and sold within Germany without a special permission, as long as it does not cause any damage on consumers' health and meets the general standards set by the legislation. However, manufacturers, carriers, importers and retailers are responsible for the food they pass into circulation. They are obliged to ensure and document the safety and quality of their food with the use of in-house control mechanisms.

Pakistan

Pakistan does not have an integrated legal framework but has a set of laws, which deals with various aspects of food safety. These laws, despite the fact that they were enacted long time ago, have tremendous capacity to achieve at least minimum level of food safety. However, like many other laws, these laws remain very poorly enforced. There are four laws that specifically deal with food safety. Three of these laws directly focus issues related to food safety, while the fourth one namely Pakistan Standards and Quality Control Authority Act, is indirectly relevant to food safety. The Pure Food Ordinance, 1960 consolidates and amends the law in relation to the preparation and the sale of foods. All provinces and some northern areas have adopted this law with certain amendments. Its aim is to ensure purity of food being supplied to people in the market and, therefore, provides for preventing adulteration. The Pure Food Ordinance 1960 does not apply to cantonment areas. There is separate law for cantonments called "The Cantonment Pure Food Act, 1966". There is no substantial difference between the Pure Food Ordinance 1960 and The Cantonment Pure Food Act. Even the rules of operation are very much similar. Pakistan Hotels and Restaurant Act, 1976 applies to all hotels and restaurants in Pakistan and seeks to control and regulate the rates and standard of service(s) by hotels and restaurants. In addition to other provisions, under section 22(2), the sale of food or beverages that are contaminated, not prepared hygienically or served in utensils that are not hygienic or clean is an offense. There are no express provisions for consumer complaints in the Pakistan Restaurants Act, 1976, Pakistan Penal Code, 1860 and Pakistan Standards and Quality Control Authority Act, 1996. However, the laws do not prevent citizens from lodging complaints with the concerned government officials. However, the consideration and handling of complaints is a matter of discretion of the officials.

South Korea

Korea Food and Drug Administration

Korea Food and Drug Administration (KFDA) is working for food safety since 1945. It is part of the Government of South Korea.

IOAS Organic Certification Bodies Registered in KFDA: 'Organic' or related claims can be labelled on food products when organic certificates are considered as valid by KFDA. KFDA admits organic certificates which can be issued by 1) IFOAM (International Federation of Organic Agriculture Movement) accredited certification bodies 2) Government accredited certification bodies - 328 bodies in 29 countries have been registered in KFDA.

Food Import Report: According to Food Import Report, it is supposed to report or register what you import. Competent authority is as followed:

- ❖ Imported Agricultural Products, Processed Foods, Food Additives, Utensils, Containers and Packages or Health Functional Foods
- ❖ KFDA (Korea Food and Drug Administration)
- ❖ Imported Livestock, Livestock products (including Dairy products)
- ❖ NVRQS (National Veterinary Research and Quarantine Service)
- ❖ Packaged meat, milk and dairy products (butter, cheese), hamburger patties, meat ball and other processed products which are stipulated by Livestock Sanitation Management Act
- ❖ Imported Marine products
- ❖ NFIS (National Fisheries Products Quality Inspection Service)
- ❖ Fresh, chilled, frozen, salted, dehydrated, eviscerated marine produce which can be recognized its characteristics.

National Institute of Food and Drug Safety Evaluation

National Institute of Food and Drug Safety Evaluation (NIFDS) is functioning as well. The National Institute of Food and Drug Safety Evaluation is a national organization for toxicological tests and research. Under the Korea Food and Drug Administration, the Institute performs research on toxicology, pharmacology, and risk analysis of foods, drugs, and their additives. The Institute strives primarily to understand important biological triggering mechanisms and improve assessment methods of human exposure, sensitivities, and risk by:

1. conducting basic, applied, and policy research that closely examines biologically triggering harmful effects on the regulated products such as foods, food additives, and drugs; and
2. operating the national toxicology programme for the toxicological test development and inspection of hazardous chemical ubstances assessments.

The Institute ensures safety by:

- investigation and research on safety by its own researchers; and
- contract research by external academicians and research centres.

The US food system is regulated by numerous federal, state and local officials. Although the US food safety system is one of the best in the world, it is lacking in "organization, regulatory tools, and resources to address food borne illness".

Federal Level Regulation

The Food and Drug Administration publishes the Food Code, a model set of guidelines and procedures that assists food control jurisdictions by providing a scientifically sound technical and legal basis for regulating the retail and food service industries, including restaurants, grocery stores and institutional foodservice providers such as nursing homes. Regulatory agencies at all levels of government in the United

States use the FDA Food Code to develop or update food safety rules in their jurisdictions that are consistent with national food regulatory policy. According to the FDA, 48 of 56 states and territories, representing 79 per cent of the U.S. population, have adopted food codes patterned after one of the five versions of the Food Code, beginning with the 1993 edition.

In the United States, federal regulations governing food safety are fragmented and complicated, according to a February 2007 report from the Government Accountability Office. There are 15 agencies sharing oversight responsibilities in the food safety system, although the two primary agencies are the U.S. Department of Agriculture (USDA) Food Safety and Inspection Service (FSIS), which is responsible for the safety of meat, poultry, and processed egg products, and the Food and Drug Administration (FDA), which is responsible for virtually all other foods.

The Food Safety and Inspection Service has approximately 7,800 inspection programme personnel working in nearly 6,200 federally inspected meat, poultry and processed egg establishments. FSIS is charged with administering and enforcing the Federal Meat Inspection Act, the Poultry Products Inspection Act, the Egg Products Inspection Act, portions of the Agricultural Marketing Act, the Humane Slaughter Act, and the regulations that implement these laws. FSIS inspection program personnel inspect every animal before slaughter, and each carcass after slaughter to ensure public health requirements are met. In fiscal year (FY) 2008, this included about 50 billion pounds of livestock carcasses, about 59 billion pounds of poultry carcasses, and about 4.3 billion pounds of processed egg products. At U.S. borders, they also inspected 3.3 billion pounds of imported meat and poultry products.

Industry Pressure

There have been concerns over the efficacy of safety practices and food industry pressure on U.S. regulators. A study reported by Reuters found that "the food industry is jeopardizing U.S. public health by withholding information from food safety investigators or pressuring regulators to withdraw or alter policy designed to protect consumers". A survey found that 25 per cent of U.S. government inspectors and scientists surveyed have experienced during the past year corporate interests forcing their food safety agency to withdraw or to modify agency policy or action that protects consumers. Scientists have observed that management undercuts field inspectors who stand up for food safety against industry pressure. According to Dr. Dean Wyatt, a USDA veterinarian who oversees federal slaughter house inspectors, "Upper level management does not adequately support field inspectors and the actions they take to protect the food supply. Not only is there lack of support, but there's outright obstruction, retaliation and abuse of power".

State and Local Regulation

A number of U.S. states have their own meat inspection programs that substitute for USDA inspection for meats that are sold only in-state. Certain state programs have been criticized for undue leniency to bad practices.

However, other state food safety programs supplement, rather than replace, Federal inspections, generally with the goal of increasing consumer confidence in the state's produce. For example, state health departments have a role in investigating outbreaks of food-borne disease bacteria, as in the case of the 2006 outbreak of *Escherichia coli* O157:H7 (bad *E. coli* bacteria) from processed spinach. Health departments also promote better food processing practices to eliminate these threats.

In addition to the US Food and Drug Administration, several states that are major producers of fresh fruits and vegetables (including California, Arizona and Florida) have their own state programmes to test produce for pesticide residues.

Restaurants and other retail food establishments fall under state law and are regulated by state or local health departments. Typically these regulations require official inspections of specific design features, best food-handling practices, and certification of food handlers. In some places a letter grade or numerical score must be prominently posted following each inspection. In some localities, inspection deficiencies and remedial action are posted on the Internet.

HACCP Guidelines

The UK Food Standards Agency publishes recommendations as part of its Hazard Analysis and Critical Control Points (HACCP) programme. The relevant guidelines state that:

❖ "Cooking food until the core temperature is 75 ºC or above will ensure that harmful bacteria are destroyed. However, lower cooking temperatures are acceptable provided that the core temperature is maintained for a specified period of time as follows:

- 60ºC for a minimum of 45 minutes
- 65ºC for a minimum of 10 minutes
- 70ºC for a minimum of 2 minutes

Previous guidance from a leaflet produced by the UK Department Of Health "Handling Cooked Meats Safely A Ten Point Plan" also allowed for:

- "75ºC for a minimum of 30 seconds
- 80ºC for a minimum of 6 seconds

Note that recommended cooking conditions are only appropriate if initial bacterial numbers in the uncooked food are small. Cooking does not overcome poor hygiene.

CONSUMER LABELLING

United Kingdom

Food stuffs in the UK have one of two labels to indicate the nature of the deterioration of the product and any subsequent health issues. EHO Food Hygiene certification is required to prepare and distribute food. While there is no specified expiry date of such a qualification the changes in legislation it is suggested to update every five years.

Best before indicates a future date beyond which the food product *may* lose quality in terms of taste or texture amongst others, but does not imply any serious health problems if food is consumed beyond this date (within reasonable limits).

Use by indicates a legal date beyond which it is not permissible to sell a food product (usually one that deteriorates fairly rapidly after production) due to the potential serious nature of consumption of pathogens. Leeway is sometimes provided by producers in stating display until dates so that products are not at their limit of safe consumption on the actual date stated (this latter is voluntary and not subject to regulatory control). This allows for the variability in production, storage and display methods.

United States

With the exception of infant formula and baby foods which must be withdrawn by their expiration date, Federal law does not require expiration dates. For all other foods, except dairy products in some states, freshness dating is strictly voluntary on the part of manufacturers. In response to consumer demand, perishable foods are typically labeled with a Sell by date. It is up to the consumer to decide how long after the Sell by date a package is usable. Other common dating statements are Best if used by, Use-by date, Expiration date, Guaranteed fresh <date>, and Pack date.

Australia and New Zealand

Guide to Food Labelling and Other Information Requirements: This guide provides background information on the general labelling requirements in the Code. The information in this guide applies both to food for retail sale and to food for catering purposes. Foods for catering purposes means those foods for use in restaurants, canteens, schools, caterers or self-catering institutions, where food is offered for immediate consumption. Labelling and information requirements in the new Code apply both to food sold or prepared for sale in Australia and New Zealand and food imported into Australia and New Zealand. Warning and Advisory Declarations, Ingredient Labelling, Date Marking, Nutrition Information Requirements, Legibility Requirements for Food Labels, Percentage Labelling, Information Requirements for Foods Exempt from Bearing a Label.

Issues Associated with Sell by/Use by Dates

According to the UK's Waste and Resources Action Programme, 33 per cent per cent of all food produced is wasted along the chill chain or at the consumer. At the same time, a large number of people get sick every year due to spoiled food.

UK Government to Replace Sell by/Use by Dates?

According to the UK minister Hilary Benn the use by date and sell by dates are old technologies that are outdated and should be replaced by other solutions or disposed of altogether.

How to Enhance Food Safety

There is a number of ways to enhance sell by and use by dates. These include better education of consumers on how to use, transport, and store fresh food products, but also by enhancing the use by and sell by dates by adding to the package smart indicators such as TTIs (Time Temperature Indicators). These show through a visible colour change whether the product is still fresh. TTIs are already in use by retailers and food producers in France (Monoprix and Carrefour), Switzerland (Kneuss), and other countries in western Europe.

Consumer Tips: How to Keep Food Safe

1. One of the simplest measures that any person can take to prevent the spread of foodborne illness is to properly wash his or her hands before preparing or eating any meal. Many people who believe they are adequately washing their hands are sorely mistaken. According to a

study conducted by the American Society of Microbiology, 97 per cent of females and 92 per cent of males said they washed their hands, but those numbers turned out to be 75 per cent of females and 58 per cent of males upon observation. A proper hand-washing technique suggested by the Missouri Department of Health and Senior Services includes using soap and warm water; washing vigorously for 10-20 seconds, making sure to reach all surfaces of the hands including the wrists, between the fingers, and under the finger nails; rinsing well; drying hands with a paper towel; and using a paper towel to turn off the water. It is certainly important to wash your hands before preparing a meal and eating, but hands should also be washed after using the restroom, coughing/sneezing, touching cuts or skin infections, handling raw meat, and touching pets or other animals. Almost half the cases of foodborne illnesses could be prevented by better hand-washing by food handlers. In addition, hand sanitizer is a helpful follow-up to hand-washing, but it should never be used to replace this valuable technique.

2. Some foods should simply never be ingested in the first place because they have such a high risk of containing harmful bacteria that can make people ill. These foods include raw milk, unpasteurized dairy products, unpasteurized juices (such as fresh apple cider), raw meat, and raw cookie dough.
3. In cases of suspected food spoilage, food should never simply be tasted, smelled, or eye-balled in order to determine its safety. It is true that in some cases, the presence of mold or other growths may indicate that a food has reached its expiration date and should not be consumed. However, some foods may look and smell fine, but if they have been stored at room temperature for over 2 hours, microscopic bacteria may have been allowed to grow. The safe temperature for foods in refrigerators is between 35°F and 45°F, and freezers should be kept at 0°F.

4. It is not safe to let meats thaw on the counter all day, because this allows any germs present on the food to thrive. Safer alternatives to this practice include thawing the food under running water (70ºF or below) for less than 2 hours, placing the food in the refrigerator to thaw, or thawing the food in the microwave as part of the cooking process.
5. It is also important to make sure that raw meats are cooked to the appropriate internal temperature before they are consumed. Safe internal temperatures for various meats include 165ºF for poultry, 155ºF for ground meat, and 145ºF for fish and pork. It is not sufficient to judge the doneness of meat by its internal color. According to a study performed by the USDA, "25 per cent of hamburgers with a brown internal color were not cooked to the proper temperature." Instead of simply eyeballing the meat, it is essential to use a meat thermometer to judge the safety of consuming the food.
6. The cooking process is often the time that foodborne pathogens are allowed to enter the food we eat because of the prevalence of cross contamination. Cross contamination occurs when a person handling raw meats, eggs, fish, or other foods containing harmful pathogens touches cooking utensils, cutting boards, or cooking surfaces and spreads the pathogens to ready-to-eat foods in the process. This mode of transmission can be interrupted by washing hands after handling raw foods, washing utensils and cutting boards that have come in contact with raw foods, and disinfecting counter surfaces frequently.
7. Leftovers are ideally stored in the refrigerator in shallow containers (2 inches tall or less) so that the cooling process can be accelerated and the buildup of harmful bacteria can be prevented. Storing foods in larger containers may keep foods warm and allow harmful bacteria to grow.

Pascalization

Pascalization, bridgmanization, or high pressure processing (HPP), is a method of preserving and sterilizing food, in which a product is processed under very high pressure, leading to the inactivation of certain microorganisms and enzymes in the food. The technique was named after Blaise Pascal, a French scientist of the 17th century whose work included detailing the effects of pressure on fluids. During pascalization, more than 50,000 pounds per square inch (340,000,000 Pa) may be applied for around fifteen minutes, leading to the inactivation of yeast, mold, and bacteria. Pascalization is also known as bridgmanization, named for physicist Percy Williams Bridgman.

Pascalization stops chemical activity caused by microorganisms that play a role in the deterioration of foods. The treatment occurs at low temperatures and does not include the use of food additives. From 1990, some juices, jellies, and jams have been preserved using pascalization in Japan. The technique is now used there to preserve fish and meats, salad dressing, rice cakes, and yogurts. An early use of pascalization in the United States was to treat guacamole. It did not change the guacamole's taste, texture, or colour, but the shelf life of the product increased to thirty days, from three days without the treatment. However, some treated foods still require cold storage because pascalization does not stop all enzyme activity caused by proteins, some of which affects shelf life.

Experiments into the effects of pressure on microorganisms have been recorded as early as 1884, and successful experiments since 1897. In 1899, B. H. Hite was the first to conclusively demonstrate the inactivation of microorganisms by pressure. After he reported the effects of high pressure on microorganisms, and reports on the effects of pressure on foods quickly followed. Hite tried to prevent milk from spoiling, and his work showed that microorganisms can be deactivated by subjecting it to high pressure. He also mentioned some advantages of pressure-treating foods, such as the lack of antiseptics and no change in taste.

Hite said that, since 1897, a chemist at the West Virginia Agricultural Experimental Station had been studying the relationship between pressure and the preservation of meats, juices, and milk. Early experiments involved inserting a large screw into a cylinder and keeping it there for several days, but this did not have any effect in stopping the milk from spoiling. Later, a more powerful apparatus was able to subject the milk to higher pressures, and the treated milk was reported to stay sweeter for 24-60 hours longer than untreated milk. When 90 short tons (82 t) of pressure was applied to samples of milk for one hour, they stayed sweet for one week. Unfortunately, the device used to induce pressure was later damaged when researchers tried to test its effects on other products.

Experiments were also performed with anthrax, typhoid, and tuberculosis, which was a potential health risk for the researchers. Indeed, before the process was improved, one employee of the Experimental Station became ill with typhoid fever.

The process that Hite reported on was not feasible for widespread use and did not always completely sterilize the milk. While more extensive investigations followed, the original study into milk was largely discontinued due to concerns over its effectiveness. Hite mentioned "certain slow changes in the milk" related to "enzymes that the pressure could not destroy".

Early 1900s

Hite *et al.* released a more detailed report on pressure sterilization in 1914, which included the number of microorganisms that remained in a product after treatment. Experiments were conducted on various other foods, including fruits, fruit juices, and some vegetables. They were met with mixed success, similar to the results obtained from the earlier tests on milk. While some foods were preserved, others were not, possibly due to bacterial spores that had not been killed.

Hite's 1914 investigation led to other studies into the effect of pressure on microorganisms. In 1918, a study published by W.P. Larson *et al.* was intended to help advance vaccines. This report showed that bacterial spores were not always inactivated by pressure, while vegetative bacteria were usually killed. Larson *et al.*'s investigation also focussed on the use of carbon dioxide, hydrogen, and nitrogen gas pressures. Carbon dioxide was found to be the most effective of the three at inactivating microorganisms.

Late 1900s–Today

Around 1970, researchers renewed their efforts in studying bacterial spores after it was discovered that using moderate pressures was more effective than using higher pressures. These spores, which caused a lack of preservation in the earlier experiments, were inactivated faster by moderate pressure, but in a manner different from what occurred with vegetative microbes. When subjected to moderate pressures, bacterial spores germinate, and the resulting spores are easily killed using pressure, heat, or ionizing radiation. If the amount of initial pressure is increased, conditions are not ideal for germination, so the original spores must be killed instead. However, using moderate pressure does not always work, as some bacterial spores are more resistant to germination under pressure and a small portion of them will survive. A preservation method using both pressure and another treatment (such as heat) to kill spores has not yet been reliably achieved. Such a technique would allow for wider use of pressure on food and other potential advancements in food preservation.

Research into the effects of high pressures on microorganisms was largely focused on deep-sea organisms until the 1980s, when advancements in ceramic processing were made.

This resulted in the production of machinery that allowed for processing foods at high pressures at a large scale, and generated some interest in the technique, especially in Japan. Although commercial products preserved by pascalization first emerged in 1990, the technology behind pascalization is still being perfected for widespread use. There is now higher demand for minimally processed products than in previous years, and products preserved by pascalization have seen commercial success despite being priced significantly higher than products treated with standard methods.

Process

In pascalization, food products are sealed and placed into a steel compartment containing a liquid, often water, and pumps are used to create pressure. The pumps may apply pressure constantly or intermittently.

The application of high hydrostatic pressures (HHP) on a food product will kill many microorganisms, but the spores of some bacteria may need to be separately treated with acid to prevent their reproduction. Pascalization works especially well on acidic foods, such as yogurts and fruits, because pressure-tolerant spores are not able to live in environments with low pH levels. The treatment works equally well for both solid and liquid products.

During pascalization, the food's proteins are denatured, hydrogen bonds are fortified, and noncovalent bonds in the food are disrupted, while the product's main structure remains intact. Because pascalization is not heat-based, covalent bonds are not affected, causing no change in the food's taste.

High hydrostatic pressure can affect muscle tissues by increasing the rate of lipid oxidation, which in turn leads to poor flavour and decreased health benefits.

Because hydrostatic pressure is able to act quickly and evenly on food, neither the size of a product's container nor its thickness play a role in the effectiveness of pascalization. There are several side effects of the process, including a slight increase in a product's sweetness, but pascalization does not greatly affect the nutritional value, taste, texture, and appearance.

As a result, high pressure treatment of foods is regarded as a 'natural' preservation method, as it does not use chemical preservatives.

Thermization

Thermization, also spelled thermisation, is a method of sterilizing raw milk with heat. The process is not used on other food products, and is similar to pasteurization but uses lower temperatures, allowing the milk product to retain more of its original taste. In Europe, there is a distinction between cheeses made of thermized milk and raw-milk cheeses.

However, the United States' Food and Drug Administration (FDA) places the same regulations on all unpasteurized cheeses. As a result, cheeses from thermized milk must be aged for 60 days or more before being sold in the United States, the same restriction placed on raw-milk cheeses by the FDA.

Thermization involves heating milk at temperatures of around 145-149°F (63-65°C) for 15 seconds, while pasteurization involves heating milk at 160°F (71°C) for 15 seconds or at 145°F (63°C) for 30 minutes.

Thermization is used to extend the keeping quality of raw milk (the length of time that milk is suitable for consumption) when it cannot be immediately used in other products, such as cheese. Thermization can also be used to extend the storage life of fermented milk products by inactivating microorganisms in the product.

Thermization inactivates psychrotrophic bacteria in milk, preventing the growth of heat-resistant enzymes and allowing the milk to be stored below 8ºC (46ºF) for three days, or stored at --1ºC (30.2ºF) for seven days.

Later, the milk may be given stronger heat treatment to be preserved longer. Cooling thermized milk before reheating it is necessary for the destruction of bacterial spores. When the milk is first heated, spores begin to germinate, but their growth is halted when the milk is refrigerated. The resulting vegetative bacteria are easier to kill with another heat treatment than the original spores.

Food Storage

Food storage is both a traditional domestic skill and is important industrially. Food is stored by almost every human society and by many animals. Storing of food has several main purposes:

- preparation for periods of scarcity or famine
- taking advantage of short term surplus of food as at harvest time
- enabling a better balanced diet throughout the year
- preparing for special events and celebrations
- planning for catastrophe or emergency
- religious reasons (LDS Church leaders council church members to store food)
- protection against predators or others

Grain

Grain is stored in rigid sealed containers to prevent ingress of moisture or attack by vermin. For domestic quantities metal cans are used (in the USA the smallest practical grain storage uses closed-top #10 metal cans).

Storage in grain sacks is not effective. Mold and pests destroy a 25 kg cloth sack of grain in a year—even if stored off the ground in a dry area. On the ground or damp concrete, the time is as little as three days, and the grain might have to be dried before it can be milled. Food stored under unsuitable conditions should not be purchased or used because of risk of spoilage. To test whether grain is still good, sprout some. If it sprouts, it is still good, but if not, it should not be eaten. It may take up to a week for grains to sprout. When in doubt, throw it out.

Meat

Unpreserved meat has only a relatively short life in storage. Pork should be eaten within one day but beef and venison improve with up to 5 days storage in a cold room. Dry aging techniques are sometimes used to tenderize specialty gourmet meats by hanging them in carefully controlled environments for up to 21 days. Semi-dried meats like salamis and country style hams are processed first with salt, smoke, sugar, or acid, or other 'cures' then hung in cool dry storage for extended periods, sometimes exceeding a year.

Fish and Shellfish

It is unsafe to store fish or shellfish without preservation. Fresh shellfish and whitefish should be eaten within a few hours of harvesting.

Use of Stored Food

Guidance for surviving emergency conditions in many parts of the world recommends maintaining a store of essential foods; typically water, cereals, oil, dried milk, and protein rich foods such as beans, lentils, tinned fish and meat. A basic food storage calculator can be used to help determine how much of these staple foods a person would need to store in order to sustain life for one full year. In addition to storing the basic food items many people choose to supplement their food storage with frozen or preserved garden-grown fruits and vegetables and freeze-dried or canned produce. An unvarying diet of staples prepared in the same way can cause appetite exhaustion.

An additional benefit to having a basic supply of food storage in the home is for the cost savings. Costs of dry bulk foods (before preparation) are often considerably less than convenience and fresh foods purchased at local markets or supermarkets.

Food Storage Rotation

If good food storage guidelines are followed, using and replenishing your food storage should become a commonplace, everyday activity, as normal as preparing meals. Although it does require an initial investment to stock a pantry, eventually it becomes the most economical and convenient way to live. Instead of going to the store when you need something and paying full price for it, you can go to your storage room or pantry to get what you need. Then you replace it next time it is on sale.

The best way to rotate your food storage is to prepare meals with it on a daily basis. Of course, that means that you should store what your family will eat. It is wasteful to store products that your family won't eat or that can't be used in your favourite recipes.

Commercial Food Storage

Grain and beans are stored in tall grain elevators, almost always at a rail head near the point of production. The grain is shipped to a final user in hopper cars. In the former Soviet Union, where harvest was poorly controlled, grain was often irradiated at the point of production to suppress mold and insects. In the U.S., threshing and drying is performed in the field, and transport is nearly sterile and in large containers that effectively suppress pest access, so irradiation is not required. At any given time, the U.S. usually has about two weeks of stored grains.

Fresh fruits and vegetables are either packed in plastic cups in cardboard boxes for fresh premium markets, or placed in large plastic tubs for sauce and soup processors. Fruits and vegetables are usually refrigerated at the earliest possible moment, and even so have a shelf life of two weeks or less.

There is a thriving but small market in bulk vegetables and convenience foods for campers.

In the USA meat animals are usually transported live, slaughtered at a major distribution point, hung and transported for two days to a week in refrigerated rail cars, and then butchered and sold locally. Before refrigerated rail cars, meat had to be transported live, and this placed its cost so high that only farmers and the wealthy could afford it every day. In Europe much meat is transported live and slaughtered close to the point of sale. In much of Africa and Asia most meat is for local populations is reared , slaughtered and eaten locally which is believed to be much less stressful for the animals involved and requires very little meat storage capacity. In Australia and New Zealand where a large proportion of meat production is for export meat is stored in very large freezer plants before being shipped overseas in freezer ships.

Food Chemistry

Food chemistry is the study of chemical processes and interactions of all biological and non-biological components of foods. The biological substances include such items as meat, poultry, lettuce, beer, and milk as examples. It is similar to biochemistry in its main components such as carbohydrates, lipids, and protein, but it also includes areas such as water, vitamins, minerals, enzymes, food additives, flavours, and colours. This discipline also encompasses how products change under certain food processing techniques and ways either to enhance or to prevent them from happening. An example of enhancing a process would be to encourage fermentation of dairy products with microorganisms that convert lactose to lactic acid; an example of preventing a process would be stopping the browning on the surface of freshly cut Red Delicious apples using lemon juice or other acidulated water.

Food chemistry's history dates back as far as the late 18th century when many famous chemists were involved in discovering chemicals important in foods, including Carl Wilhelm Scheele (isolated malic acid from apples in 1785), and

Sir Humphry Davy published the first ever book on agricultural and food chemistry in 1813 titled *Elements of Agricultural Chemistry, in a Course of Lectures for the Board of Agriculture* in the United Kingdom which would serve as a foundation for the profession worldwide, going into a fifth edition.

In 1874 the Society of Public Analysts was formed, with the aim of applying analytical methods to the benefit of the public . Its early experiments were based on bread, milk and wine.

It was also out of concern for the quality of the food supply, mainly food adulteration and contamination issues that would first stem from intentional contamination to later with chemical food additives by the 1950s. The development of colleges and universities worldwide, most notably in the United States, would expand food chemistry as well with research of the dietary substances, most notably the Single-grain experiment during 1907-11. Additional research by Harvey W. Wiley at the United States Department of Agriculture during the late 19th century would play a key factor in the creation of the United States Food and Drug Administration in 1906. The American Chemical Society would establish their Agricultural and Food Chemistry Division in 1908 while the Institute of Food Technologists would establish their Food Chemistry Division in 1995.

Water

A major component of food is water, which can encompass anywhere from 50 per cent in meat products to 95 per cent in lettuce, cabbage, and tomato products. It is also an excellent place for bacterial growth and food spoilage if it is not properly processed. One way this is measured in food is by water activity which is very important in the shelf life of many foods during processing. One of the keys to food preservation in most instances is reduce the amount of water or alter the water's characteristics to enhance shelf-life. Such methods include dehydration, freezing, and refrigeration.

Carbohydrates

Comprising 75 per cent of the biological world and 80 per cent of all food intake for human consumption, the most common known human carbohydrate is starch. The simplest version of a carbohydrate is a monosaccharide which possesses the properties of carbon, hydrogen, and oxygen in a 1:2:1 ratio under a general formula of $C_nH_{2n}O_n$ where *n* is a minimum of 3. Glucose is an example of a monosaccharide as is fructose. Combine them in the picture shown to the right and you have sucrose, one of the more common sugar products around.

A chain of monosaccharides form to make a polysaccharide. Such polysaccharides include pectin, dextran, agar, and xanthan.

Sugar content is commonly measured in degrees brix.

Lipids

The term lipid comprises a diverse range of molecules and to some extent is a catchall for relatively water-insoluble or non-polar compounds of biological origin, including waxes, fatty acids (including essential fatty acids), fatty-acid derived phospholipids, sphingolipids, glycolipids and terpenoids, such as retinoids and steroids. Some lipids are linear aliphatic molecules, while others have ring structures. Some are aromatic, while others are not. Some are flexible, while others are rigid.

Most lipids have some polar character in addition to being largely nonpolar. Generally, the bulk of their structure is nonpolar or hydrophobic ('water-fearing'), meaning that it does not interact well with polar solvents like water. Another part of their structure is polar or hydrophilic ('water-loving') and will tend to associate with polar solvents like water. This makes them amphiphilic molecules (having both hydrophobic and hydrophilic portions). In the case of cholesterol, the polar group is a mere -OH (hydroxyl or alcohol).

Lipids in food include the oils of such grains as corn, soybean, from animal fats, and are parts of many foods such as milk, cheese, and meat. They also act as vitamin carriers as well.

Proteins

Proteins compose over 50 per cent of the dry weight of an average living cell and are very complex macromolecules. They also play a fundamental role in the structure and function of cells. Consisting mainly of carbon, nitrogen, hydrogen, oxygen, and some sulfur, they also may contain iron, copper, phosphorus, or zinc.

In food, proteins are essential for growth and survival and vary depending upon a person's age and physiology (*e.g.*, pregnancy). Proteins in food are commonly found in peanuts, meat, poultry, and seafood. They are also involved in ELISA test for food allergy determination.

Enzymes

Enzymes are biochemical catalysts used in converting processes from one substance to another. They are also involved in reducing the amount of time and energy required to complete a chemical process. Many aspects of the food industry use catalysts, including baking, brewing, dairy, and fruit juices, to make cheese, beer, and bread.

Vitamins

Vitamins are nutrients required in small amounts for essential metabolic reactions in the body. These are broken down in nutrition as either water soluble (Vitamin C) or fat soluble (Vitamin E). An adequate supply of vitamins can prevent diseases such as beriberi, anemia, and scurvy while an overdose of vitamins can produce nausea and vomiting or even death.

Minerals

Dietary minerals in foods are large and diverse with many required to function while other trace elements can be hazardous if consumed in excessive amounts. Bulk minerals with a Reference Daily Intake (RDI, formerly Recommended Daily Allowance (RDA)) of more than 200 mg/day are calcium, magnesium, and potassium while important trace minerals (RDI less than 200 mg/day) are copper, iron, and zinc. These are found in many foods, but can also be taken in dietary supplements.

Colour

Food colouring is added to change the colour of any food substance. It is mainly for sensory analysis purposes. It can be used to simulate the natural colour of a product as perceived by the customer, such as red dye like FD & C Red No. 40 (Allura Red AC) to ketchup or to add unnatural colours to a product like Kellogg's Froot Loops. Caramel is a natural food dye; the industrial form, caramel colouring, is the most widely-used food colouring and is found in foods from soft drinks to soy sauce, bread, and pickles.

Flavours

Flavour in food is important in how food smells and tastes to the consumer, especially in sensory analysis. Some of these products occur naturally like salt and sugar, but flavour chemists (called a 'flavourist') develop many of these flavours for food products. Such artificial flavours include methyl salicylate which creates the wintergreen odour and lactic acid which gives milk a tart taste.

Food Additives

Food additives are substances added to food for preserving flavours, or improving taste or appearance. These processes are as old as adding vinegar for pickling or as an emulsifier for emulsion mixtures like mayonnaise. These are generally listed by 'E number' in the European Union or GRAS ("generally recognized as safe") by the United States Food and Drug Administration.

Convenience Food

Convenience food, or tertiary processed food, is commercially prepared food designed for ease of consumption. Products designated as convenience foods are often prepared food stuffs that can be sold as hot, ready-to-eat dishes; as room-temperature, shelf-stable products; or as refrigerated or frozen products that require minimal preparation (typically just heating).

These products are often sold in portion controlled, single serve packaging designed for portability for 'on-the-go' eating. Convenience food can include products such as candy; beverages such as soft drinks, juices and milk; fast food; nuts, fruits and vegetables in fresh or preserved states; processed meats and cheeses; and canned products such as soups and pasta dishes.

Modern convenience food saw its beginnings in the period that began after World War II in the United States. Many of these products had their origins in military developed foods ,designed for storage longevity and ease of preparation in the battle field. After the war, many commercial food companies were left with surplus manufacturing facilities. These companies developed new lines of canned and freeze dried foods that were designed for use in the home. Like many product introductions, not all were successful—convenience food staples such as fish sticks and canned peaches were counterbalanced by failures such as ham sticks and cheeseburgers-in-a-can.

Criticisms

Critics have derided the increasing trend of convenience foods because of numerous issues. Several groups have cited the environmental harm of single serve packaging due to the increased usage of plastics that contributes to solid waste in landfills.

Nutritional Issues

According to a page on the website of the Cleveland Clinic: "Most convenience foods on the market today are laden with saturated fats, sodium and sugar and provide little to no nutritional value".

Salt

Salt is an essential nutrient, but sodium, usually in the form of salt has been linked with high blood pressure. A single serving of many convenience foods contains a significant portion of the recommended daily allowance of sodium. Manufacturers are concerned that if the taste of each product is not optimized by adding salt that it will not sell as well as competing products. Tests have shown that some popular packaged foods are dependent on significant amounts of salt for their palatability.

Labelling, Mitigation, and Regulation

In response to the issues surrounding the healthfulness of convenience and restaurant foods, an initiative in the United States, spearheaded by first lady Michelle Obama and her 'Let's Move' campaign, to reduce the unhealthy aspects of commercially produced food and fight childhood obesity, was unveiled by the White House in February 2010. Using her position as a bully pulpit, Mrs. Obama has pushed the industry to cut back on sugars and salts found in many convenience foods, encouraging self regulation over government intervention through laws and regulations. Despite Mrs. Obama's stated preference on self-regulation, the Food and Drug Administration announced that it was looking into quantifying the guidelines into law while other groups and municipalities are seeking to add other preventative measures such as target taxes and levies onto these products. In response to the attention, in April 2010 a coalition of sixteen manufactures all agreed to reduce salt levels in foods sold in the United States under a programme based on a similar effort in the United Kingdom. However, the initiative has met with resistance from some manufacturers, who claim that processed foods require the current high levels of salt to remain appetizing and to mask undesirable effects of food processing such as "warmed over flavour." The coalition expanded its mission in May 2010 by announcing that it intends to reduce the amount of calories in foods. By introducing lower calorie foods, changing product recipes and reducing portion sizes, the coalition stated that it expected to reduce the caloric content of foods by more than 1.5 trillion calories in total by 2012.

17 Fast Food

A typical fast food meal in the Big Ass Boner United States consists of french fries and a hamburger (or other main item). Fast food (also known as Quick Service Restaurant or QSR within the industry itself) is the term given to food that can be prepared and served very quickly. While any meal with low preparation time can be considered to be fast food, typically the term refers to food sold in a restaurant or store with preheated or precooked ingredients, and served to the customer in a packaged form for take-out/take-away. The term 'fast food' was recognized in a dictionary by Merriam–Webster in 1951.

Outlets may be stands or kiosks, which may provide no shelter or seating, or fast food restaurants (also known as *quick service restaurants*). Franchise operations which are part of restaurant chains have standardized foodstuffs shipped to each restaurant from central locations.

The capital requirements involved in opening up a non-franchised fast food restaurant are relatively low. Restaurants with much higher sit-in ratios, where customers tend to sit and have their orders brought to them in a seemingly more upscale atmosphere, may be known in some areas as fast casual restaurants.

In Ancient Rome cities had street stands that sold bread and wine. A fixture of East Asian cities is the noodle shop. Flatbread and falafel are today ubiquitous in the Middle East. Popular Indian fast food dishes include vada pav, panipuri and dahi vada. In the French-speaking nations of West Africa, roadside stands in and around the larger cities continue to sell—as they have done for generations—a range of ready-to-eat, char-grilled meat sticks known locally as *brochettes* (not to be confused with the bread snack of the same name found in Europe).

In the cities of Roman antiquity, much of the urban population living in *insulae,* multi-storey apartment blocks, depended on food vendors for much of their meals. In the mornings, bread soaked in wine was eaten as a quick snack and cooked vegetables and stews later in the day at a *popina,* a simple type of eating establishment. In the Middle Ages, large towns and major urban areas such as London and Paris supported numerous vendors that sold dishes such as pies, pasties, flans, waffles, wafers, pancakes and cooked meats. As in Roman cities during antiquity, many of these establishments catered to those who did not have means to cook their own food, particularly single households. Unlike richer town dwellers, many could often not afford housing with kitchen facilities and thus relied on fast food. Travellers, as well, such as pilgrims en route to a holy site, were among the customers.

In areas which had access to coastal or tidal waters, 'fast food' would frequently include local shellfish or seafood, such as oysters or, as in London, eels. Often this seafood would be cooked directly on the quay or close by. The development of trawler fishing in the mid nineteenth century would lead to the development of a British favourite fish and chips partly due to such activities.

British fast food had considerable regional variation. Sometimes the regionality of dish became part of the culture of its respective area.

The content of fast food pies has varied, with poultry (such as chickens) or wildfowl commonly being used. After World War II, turkey has been used more frequently in fast food.

A particularly British form of fast food is the sandwich, popularised by John Montagu, the fourth Earl of Sandwich in 1762 when he wrapped dried meat in bread so as not to interrupt his work or his gambling (accounts vary). The sandwich has similarities in other cuisines and cultures such as the filled baguettes popular in France. Despite its wide appeal and consumption in the UK, it is only in recent years that the sandwich in its various forms has been considered to be fast food, initially being promoted as such by niche chains such as Subway and Pret a Manger.

As well as its native forms, the UK has adopted fast food from other cultures, such as pizza (Italian), Chinese noodles, kebab, curry and various other forms of fast foods come from other parts of the Commonwealth of Nations. And further afield. In some areas imported fast food has become part of both the local, and British culture in general. More recently healthier alternatives to conventional fast food have also emerged.

A 2008 study was conducted worldwide counting the number of fast food restaurants per person.The UK has claimed this title with Australia second and the United States third. England alone accounted for 25 per cent of all fast food.

As automobiles became popular and affordable following the First World War, drive-in restaurants were introduced. The American company White Castle, founded by Billy Ingram and Walter Anderson in Wichita, Kansas in 1921, is generally credited with opening the second fast food outlet and first hamburger chain, selling hamburgers for five cents each. Walter Anderson had built the first White Castle restaurant in Wichita in 1916, introducing the limited menu, high volume, low cost, high speed hamburger restaurant. Among its innovations, the company allowed customers to see the food being prepared. White Castle was successful from its inception and spawned numerous competitors.

Franchising was introduced in 1921 by A&W Root Beer, which franchised its distinctive syrup. Howard Johnson's first franchised the restaurant concept in the mid-1930s, formally standardizing menus, signage and advertising.

Curb service was introduced in the late 1920s and was mobilized in the 1940s when carhops strapped on roller skates.

The United States has the largest fast food industry in the world, and American fast food restaurants are located in over 100 countries. Approximately 2 million U.S. workers are employed in the areas of food preparation and food servicing including fast food in the USA.

Fast food outlets are *take-away* or *take-out* providers, often with a 'drive-through' service which allows customers to order and pick up food from their cars; but most also have a seating area in which customers can eat the food on the premises.

Nearly from its inception, fast food has been designed to be eaten 'on the go', often does not require traditional cutlery, and is eaten as a finger food. Common menu items at fast food outlets include fish and chips, sandwiches, pitas, hamburgers, fried chicken, french fries, chicken nuggets, tacos, pizza, hot dogs, and ice cream, although many fast food restaurants offer 'slower' foods like chili, mashed potatoes, and salads.

Filling Stations

Many petrol/gas stations have convenience stores which sell pre-packaged sandwiches, doughnuts, and hot food. Many gas stations in the United States also sell frozen foods and have microwaves on the premises in which to prepare them.

Traditional street food is available around the world, usually from small operators and independent vendors operating from a cart, table, portable grill or motor vehicle. Common examples include Vietnamese noodle vendors,

Middle Eastern falafel stands, New York City hot dog carts, and taco trucks. Turo-Turo vendors (Tagalog for point point) are a feature of Philippine life. Commonly, street vendors provide a colourful and varying range of options designed to quickly captivate passers-by and attract as much attention as possible.

Depending on the locale, multiple street vendors may specialize in specific types of food characteristic of a given cultural or ethnic tradition. In some cultures, it is typical for street vendors to call out prices, sing or chant sales-pitches, play music, or engage in other forms of 'street theatrics' in order to engage prospective customers. In some cases, this can garner more attention than the food itself; some vendors represent another form of tourist attraction.

Cuisine

Modern commercial fast food is often highly processed and prepared in an industrial fashion, *i.e.*, on a large scale with standard ingredients and standardized cooking and production methods. It is usually rapidly served in cartons or bags or in a plastic wrapping, in a fashion which minimizes cost. In most fast food operations, menu items are generally made from processed ingredients prepared at a central supply facility and then shipped to individual outlets where they are reheated, cooked (usually by microwave or deep frying) or assembled in a short amount of time. This process ensures a consistent level of product quality, and is key to being able to deliver the order quickly to the customer and eliminate labour and equipment costs in the individual stores.

Because of commercial emphasis on speed, uniformity and low cost, fast food products are often made with ingredients formulated to achieve a certain flavour or consistency and to preserve freshness.

Although fast food often brings to mind traditional American fast food such as hamburgers and fries, there are many other forms of fast food that enjoy widespread popularity in the West.

Chinese takeaways/takeout restaurants are particularly popular. They normally offer a wide variety of Asian food (not always Chinese), which has normally been fried. Most options are some form of noodles, rice, or meat. In some cases, the food is presented as a smörgåsbord, sometimes self service. The customer chooses the size of the container they wish to buy, and then is free to fill it with their choice of food. It is common to combine several options in one container, and some outlets charge by weight rather than by item. Many of these restaurants offer free delivery for purchases over a minimum amount.

Sushi has seen rapidly rising popularity in recent times. A form of fast food created in Japan (where bento is the Japanese equivalent of fast food), sushi is normally cold sticky rice flavoured with a sweet rice vinegar and served with some topping (often fish), or, as in the most popular kind in the West, rolled in nori (dried laver) with filling. The filling often includes fish, chicken or cucumber.

Pizza is a common fast food category in the United States, with chains such as Papa John's, Domino's Pizza, Sbarro and Pizza Hut. Menus are more limited and standardized than in traditional pizzerias, and pizza delivery, often with a time commitment, is offered.

Kebab houses are a form of fast food restaurant from the Middle East, especially Turkey and Lebanon. Meat is shaven from a rotisserie, and is served on a warmed flatbread with salad and a choice of sauce and dressing. These doner kebabs or shawarmas are distinct from shish kebabs served on sticks. Kebab shops are also found throughout the world, especially Europe, New Zealand and Australia but they generally are less common in the US.

Fish and chip shops are a form of fast food popular in the United Kingdom, Australia and New Zealand. Fish is battered and then deep fried.

The Dutch have their own types of fast food. A Dutch fast food meal often consists of a portion of french fries (called friet or patat) with a sauce and a meat product. The most common sauce to accompany french fries is mayonnaise, while others can be ketchup or spiced ketchup, peanut sauce or piccalilli. Sometimes the fries are served with combinations of sauces, most famously *speciaal* (special): mayonnaise, with (spiced) ketchup and chopped onions; and *oorlog* (literally 'war'): mayonnaise and peanut sauce (sometimes also with ketchup and chopped onions). The meat product is usually a deep fried snack; this includes the frikandel (a deep fried skinless minced meat sausage), and the kroket (deep fried meat ragout covered in breadcrumbs).

In Portugal, there are some varieties of local fast-food and restaurants specialized in this type of local cuisine. Some of the most popular foods include the popular *frango assado* (Piri-piri grilled chicken previously marinated), francesinha, francesinha poveira, espetada (succulent turkey or pork meat on two sticks) and bifanas (pork cutlets in a specific sauce served as a sandwich).

This type of food is also often served with french fries (called *batatas fritas*), some international chains started appearing specialized in some of the typical Portuguese fast food such as Nando's.

In the United States alone, consumers spent about US$110 billion on fast food in 2000 (which increased from US$6 billion in 1970). The National Restaurant Association forecasted that fast food restaurants in the U.S. would reach US$142 billion in sales in 2006, a 5 per cent increase over 2005.

In comparison, the full-service restaurant segment of the food industry is expected to generate $173 billion in sales. Fast food has been losing market share to fast casual dining restaurants, which offer more robust and expensive cuisines.

In 2006, the global fast food market grew by 4.8 per cent and reached a value of 102.4 billion and a volume of 80.3 billion transactions. In India alone the fast food industry is growing by 41 per cent a year.

McDonald's is located in 126 countries and on 6 continents and operates over 31,000 restaurants worldwide. On January 31, 1990 McDonald's opened a restaurant in Moscow, and broke opening day records for customers served.

The Moscow restaurant is the busiest in the world. The largest McDonald's in the world is located in Beijing, People's Republic of China.

There are numerous other fast food restaurants located all over the world. Burger King has more than 11,100 restaurants in more than 65 countries. KFC is located in 25 countries. Subway is one of the fastest growing franchises in the world with approximately 39,129 restaurants in 90 countries as of May 2009, the first non-US location opening in December 1984 in Bahrain. Pizza Hut is located in 97 countries, with 100 locations in China. Taco Bell has 278 restaurants located in 12 countries besides the United States.

Fast food chains have come under fire from consumer groups, such as the Center for Science in the Public Interest, a longtime fast food critic over issues such as caloric content, trans fats and portion sizes. In 2001, Eric Schlosser's investigative work *Fast Food Nation* provided Americans with a detailed look at the culture of fast food from rangeland to the range top. In 2008, Caesar Barber attempted to sue a number of fast food restaurant chains for making him obese.

The suit never went to court. Social scientists have highlighted how the prominence of fast food narratives in popular urban legends suggests that modern consumers have an ambivalent relationship (characterized by guilt) with fast food, particularly in relation to children. This guilt is projected onto processed food, where bizarre tales of contamination and lax standards are widely believed.

Some of the concerns have led to the rise of the Slow Food, or local food movements. These movements seek to preserve local cuisines and ingredients, and directly oppose laws and habits that favour fast food choices.

Proponents of the slow food movement try to educate consumers about what its members considers the richer, more varied and more nourishing tastes of fresh, local ingredients that have been recently harvested.

In Japan, the emphasis is instead on education about food nutrition and production, called shokuiku. The government does not campaign against personal decisions but ensures that every citizen understands where their food comes from.

According to the Massachusetts Medical Society Committee on Nutrition, fast food is especially high in fat content, and studies have found associations between fast food intake and increased body mass index (BMI) and weight gain. A 2006 study fed monkeys a diet consisting of a similar level of trans fats as what a person who ate fast food regularly would consume. Both diets contained the same overall number of calories.

It was found that the monkeys who consumed higher level of trans fat developed more abdominal fat than those fed a diet rich in unsaturated fats. They also developed signs of insulin resistance, which is an early indicator of diabetes. After six years on the diet, the trans fat fed monkeys had gained 7.2 per cent of their body weight, compared to just 1.8 per cent in the unsaturated fat group.

The director of the obesity programme for the Children's Hospital Boston, David Ludwig, claims that "fast food consumption has been shown to increase calorie intake, promote weight gain, and elevate risk for diabetes". The Centres for Disease Control and Prevention ranked obesity as the number one health threat for Americans in 2003.

It is the second leading cause of preventable death in the United States and results in 400,000 deaths each year. About 60 million American adults are classified as being obese with another 127 million being overweight. Health issues associated with obesity causes economic despair regarding health care. According to a 2003 study conducted by RTI International in North Carolina, the cost of health care in

America is said to increase by $93 billion a year, mainly from Type 2 diabetes and heart disease, both associated with obesity.

Excessive calories are another issue with fast food. According to B. Lin and E. Frazao, from the Department of Agriculture, states the percentage of calories which attribute to fast-food consumption has increased from 3 per cent to 12 per cent of the total calories consumed in the United States. A regular meal at McDonald's consists of a Big Mac, large fries, and a large Coca-Cola drink amounting to 1,430 calories. A diet of approximately 2,000 calories is considered a healthy amount of calories for an entire day (which is different depending on several factors such as age, weight, height, physical activity and gender).

Besides the dangers of trans fats, high calories, and low fiber, there is another health risk: food poisoning. In his book *Fast Food Nation: The Dark Side of the All-American Meal*, Eric Schlosser describes in gross detail the process of meatpacking. Meatpacking has become one of the most hazardous jobs in America, with the risk of injury being three times higher than any other factory work. The meatpacking factories concentrate livestock into large feedlots and herd them through processing assembly lines operated by poorly trained employees increase the risk of large-scale food poisoning. Manure gets mixed with meat, contaminating it with salmonella and *Escherichia coli* 0157:H7. *E. coli* 0157:H7 is one of the worst forms of food poisoning. Usually spread through undercooked hamburgers, it is difficult to treat.

Although antibiotics kill the bacteria, they release a toxin that produces hurtful complications. About 4 per cent of people infected with *E. coli* 0157:H7 develop hemolytic uremic syndrome, and about 5 per cent of children who develop the syndrome die. *E. coli* 0157:H7 has become the leading cause of renal failure among American kids.

In a research experiment done by Paediatrics, 6,212 children and adolescents ages 4 to 19 years old were examined to find out some information about fast food. After interviewing the participants in the experiment, it was discovered that on a given day 30.3 per cent of the total sample have reported to have eaten fast food. Fast-food consumption was prevalent in both males and females, all racial/ethnic groups, and all regions of the country.

Children who ate fast food, compared with those who did not, consumed more total fat, carbohydrates, and sugar-sweetened beverages. Children who ate fast food also ate less fiber, milk, fruits, and non-starchy vegetables. After reviewing these test results, the researchers concluded that consumption of fast food by children seems to have a negative effect on an individual's diet, in ways that could significantly increase the risk for obesity. On average nearly one-third of U.S children aged 4 to 19 eat fast food on a daily basis. Over the course of a year this bad habit is likely to result in the child gaining six extra pounds every year.

Caesar Barber Controversy

Caesar Barber (born 1945) is an American man who became famous for his attempts to sue the fast food chains McDonalds, Burger King, Wendy's, and KFC for having made him addicted to their foods, resulting in his becoming overweight.

At the time of the suit, Barber was 57 years old and weighed 272 pounds (123 kilograms). He was medically obese, suffered from diabetes, and had two heart attacks. He lived in the Bronx, and worked as a maintenance worker. Over a period of years, he ate fast food four to five times each week.

"I trace all [my health problems] back to the high fat, grease and salt, all back to McDonald's, Wendy's, Burger King - there was no fast food I didn't eat, and I ate it more often than not because I was single, it was quick and I'm not a very good cook. It was a necessity, and I think it was killing me, my doctor said it was killing me, and I don't want to die."

His lawyer, Samuel Hirsch, hoped to qualify for class action status, which would have had allowed him to sue on behalf of all overweight people in New York state, and perhaps nationally. In so far as more than 30 per cent of Americans are overweight, 30 per cent of that are obese, and more than half eat at McDonald's regularly, the potential judgment was enormous.

Hirsch called McDonald's, Burger King, Wendy's and KFC Corporation irresponsible and deceptive in the posting of their nutritional information. He railed that they need to offer healthier options on their menus, and that they create a *de facto* addiction in their consumers, particularly the poor and children.

"You don't need nicotine or an illegal drug to create an addiction, you're creating a craving. I think we'll find that the fast-food industry has not been totally up front with the consumers".

The lawsuit didn't ask for a particular amount of money, and ultimately never made it to court.

Food-contact Paper Packaging

Fast food often comes in wrappers coated with perfluoroalkyls (PAC) to prevent grease from leaking through them. These have been proven to get into the human body. PAC changes to a more harmful form inside the human body and can cause numerous health problems. The United State's National Institute of Health stated that while other sources of this pollutant exist, the wrappers should be "considered as a significant indirect source of human PFCA contamination".

18 Food Microbiology

Food microbiology is the study of the microorganisms that inhabit, create, or contaminate food. Of major importance is the study of microorganisms causing food spoilage. 'Good' bacteria, however, such as probiotics, are becoming increasingly important in food science. In addition, microorganisms are essential for the production of foods such as cheese, yogurt, other fermented foods, bread, beer and wine.

Food Safety

Food safety is a major focus of food microbiology. Pathogenic bacteria, viruses and toxins produced by microorganisms are all possible contaminants of food. However, microorganisms and their products can also be used to combat these pathogenic microbes. Probiotic bacteria, including those that produce bacteriocins, can kill and inhibit pathogens. Alternatively, purified bacteriocins such as nisin can be added directly to food products. Finally, bacteriophages, viruses that only infect bacteria, can be used to kill bacterial pathogens. Thorough preparation of food, including proper cooking, eliminates most bacteria and viruses. However, toxins produced by contaminants may not be heat-labile, and some are not eliminated by cooking.

Fermentation

Fermentation is one way microorganisms can change a food. Yeast, especially *Saccharomyces cerevisiae,* is used to leaven bread, brew beer and make wine. Certain bacteria, including lactic acid bacteria, are used to make yogurt, cheese, hot sauce, pickles, fermented sausages and dishes such as kimchi. A common effect of these fermentations is that the food product is less hospitable to other microorganisms, including pathogens and spoilage-causing microorganisms, thus extending the food's shelf-life.

Food fermentations are ancient technologies that harness microorganisms and their enzymes to improve the human diet. Fermented foods keep better, have enhanced flavours, textures and aromas, and may also possess certain health benefits, including superior digestibility. For vegetarians, fermented foods serve as palatable, protein-rich meat substitutes.

Some cheese varieties also require molds to ripen and develop their characteristic flavours.

Asian cuisines rely on a large repertoire of fermented foods. In particular, *Aspergillus oryzae* and *A. sojae,* sometimes called koji molds, are employed in many ways. Their hydrolytic enzymes suit them for growth on starch and other carbohydrate-rich substrates. In the koji process, fungal enzymes perform the same function as the malting enzymes used in the beer fermentations of western cultures.

The koji molds release amylases that break down rice starch, which in turn can be fermented to make rice wine. Fermented rice beverages have numerous local variations and names, depending on country and region. Rice wine is called *shaoshing* in parts of China, *sake* in Japan, *takj* or *yakju* in Korea, as well as by many other names across Asia.

The koji molds are also effective in a variety of legume fermentations, of which miso and soy sauce are best known. Miso is a mixture of soybeans and cereals usually used to flavour soups. Soy sauce is a flavourful, salty liquid sauce made from soybeans that have been fermented by koji molds, yeasts, as well as several halophilic bacteria. Other names for soy sauce include *jiangyou* (China), *makjang* and *kanjang* (Korea), *toyo* (Philippines) and *siiu* (Thailand).

Probiotics

Probiotics are living organisms that, when consumed, have beneficial health benefits outside their inherent nutritional effects. There is a growing body of evidence for the role of probiotics in gastrointestinal infections, irritable bowel syndrome and inflammatory bowel disease.

Lactobacillus species are used for the production of yogurt, cheese, sauerkraut, pickles, beer, wine, cider, kimchi, chocolate and other fermented foods, as well as animal feeds such as silage.

In recent years, much interest has been shown in the use of lactobacilli as probiotic organisms and their potential for disease prevention in humans and animals.

Bifidobacteria are considered as important probiotics, and are used in the food industry to relieve and treat many intestinal disorders. Bifidobacteria exert a range of beneficial health effects, including the regulation of intestinal microbial homeostasis, the inhibition of pathogens and harmful bacteria that colonize and/or infect the gut mucosa, the modulation of local and systemic immune responses, the repression of procarcinogenic enzymatic activities within the microbiota, the production of vitamins, and the bioconversion of a number of dietary compounds into bioactive molecules.

Microbial Biopolymers

A variety of biopolymers, such as polysaccharides, polyesters and polyamides, are naturally produced by microorganisms. Several microbially-produced polymers are used in the food industry.

Xanthan

Plant-pathogenic bacteria of the genus *Xanthomonas* are able to produce the acidic exopolysaccharide xanthan gum.

Because of its physical properties, it is widely used as a viscosifer, thickener, emulsifier or stabilizer in the food industry. Xanthan consists of pentasaccharide repeat units composed of D-glucosyl, D-mannosyl, and D-glucuronyl acid residues in a molar ratio of 2:2:1 and variable proportions of O-acetyl and pyruvyl residues.

Alginate

Alginate is the main representative of a family of polysaccharides that neither show branching nor repeating blocks or unit patterns and this property distinguishes it from to other polymers like xanthan or dextran.

Alginates can be used as thickening agents. Although listed here under the category 'Microbial polysaccharides', commercial alginates are currently only produced by extraction from brown seaweeds such as *Laminaria hyperborea* or *L. japonica*.

Cellulose

Cellulose is a simple polysaccharide, in that it consists only of one type of sugar (glucose), and the units are linearly arranged and linked together by ß-1,4 linkages only.

The mechanism of biosynthesis is, however, rather complex, partly because in native celluloses, the chains are organized as highly ordered water-insoluble fibers. Currently, the key genes involved in cellulose biosynthesis and regulation are known in a number of bacteria, but many details of the biochemistry of its biosynthesis are still not clear. In spite of the enormous abundance of cellulose in plants, bacterial celluloses are being investigated for industrial exploitations.

Poly-glutamic Acid

Poly-glutamic acid (?-PGA) produced by various strains of *Bacillus* has potential applications as a thickener in the food industry.

Levan

Levan, a homopolysaccharide composed of D-fructofuranosyl residues joined by 2,6 with multiple branches by 2, 1 linkages, has great potential as a functional biopolymer in foods, feeds, cosmetics, and the pharmaceutical and chemical industries. Levan can be used as food or a feed additive with prebiotic and hypocholesterolemic effects.

Exopolysaccharides

Microorganisms synthesize a wide spectrum of multifunctional polysaccharides, including intracellular polysaccharides, structural polysaccharides and extracellular polysaccharides or exopolysaccharides (EPSs). EPSs generally consist of monosaccharides and some non-carbohydrate substituents (such as acetate, pyruvate, succinate, and phosphate). Owing to the wide diversity in composition, they have found multifarious applications in various food and pharmaceutical industries.

Foodborne Pathogens

Foodborne pathogens are the leading causes of illness and death in less developed countries, killing approximately 1.8 million people annually. In developed countries, foodborne pathogens are responsible for millions of cases of infectious gastrointestinal diseases each year, costing billions of dollars in medical care and lost productivity.

New foodborne pathogens and foodborne diseases are likely to emerge, driven by factors such as pathogen evolution, changes in agricultural and food manufacturing practices, and changes to the human host status. There are growing concerns that terrorists could use pathogens to contaminate food and water supplies in attempts to incapacitate thousands of people and disrupt economic growth.

Enteric Viruses

Food and waterborne viruses contribute to a substantial number of illnesses throughout the world. Among those most commonly known are hepatitis A virus, rotavirus, astrovirus, enteric adenovirus, hepatitis E virus, and the human caliciviruses consisting of the noroviruses and the Sapporo viruses. This diverse group is transmitted by the fecal-oral route, often by ingestion of contaminated food and water.

Protozoan Parasites

Protozoan parasites associated with food and water can cause illness in humans. Although parasites are more commonly found in developing countries, developed countries have also experienced several foodborne outbreaks.

Contaminants may be inadvertently introduced to the foods by inadequate handling practices, either on the farm or during processing of foods. Protozoan parasites can be found worldwide, either infecting wild animals or in water and contaminating crops grown for human consumption. The disease can be much more severe and prolonged in immuno-compromissed individuals.

Mycotoxins

Molds produce mycotoxins, which are secondary metabolites that can cause acute or chronic diseases in humans when ingested from contaminated foods. Potential diseases include cancers and tumors in different organs (heart, liver, kidney, nerves), gastrointestinal disturbances, alteration of the immune system, and reproductive problems.

Species of *Aspergillus, Fusarium, Penicillium,* and *Claviceps* grow in agricultural commodities or foods and produce the mycotoxins such as aflatoxins, deoxynivalenol, ochratoxin A, fumonisins, ergot alkaloids, T-2 toxin, and zearalenone and other minor mycotoxins such as cyclopiazonic acid and patulin.

Mycotoxins occur mainly in cereal grains (barley, maize, rye, wheat), coffee, dairy products, fruits, nuts and spices. Control of mycotoxins in foods has focused on minimizing mycotoxin production in the field, during storage or destruction once produced. Monitoring foods for mycotoxins is important to manage strategies such as regulations and guidelines, which are used by 77 countries, and for developing exposure assessments essential for accurate risk characterization.

Aflatoxins are still recognized as the most important mycotoxins. They are synthesized by only a few *Aspergillus* species, of which *A. flavus* and *A. parasiticus* are the most problematic. The expression of aflatoxin-related diseases is influenced by factors such as age, nutrition, sex, species and the possibility of concurrent exposure to other toxins.

The main target organ in mammals is the liver, so aflatoxicosis is primarily a hepatic disease. Conditions increasing the likelihood of aflatoxicosis in humans include limited availability of food, environmental conditions that favour mold growth on foodstuffs, and lack of regulatory systems for aflatoxin monitoring and control.

Yersinia Enterocolitica

Yersinia enterocolitica includes pathogens and environmental strains that are ubiquitous in terrestrial and fresh water ecosystems. Evidence from large outbreaks of yersiniosis and from epidemiological studies of sporadic cases has shown that *Y. enterocolitica* is a foodborne pathogen. Pork is often implicated as the source of infection.

The pig is the only animal consumed by man that regularly harbours pathogenic *Y. enterocolitica*. An important property of the bacterium is its ability to multiply at temperatures near 0ºC, and therefore in many chilled foods. The pathogenic serovars (mainly O:3, O:5,27, O:8 and O:9) show different geographical distribution. However, the appearance of strains of serovars O:3 and O:9 in Europe, Japan in the 1970s, and in North America by the end of the 1980s, is an example of a global pandemic. There is a possible risk of reactive arthritis following infection with *Y. enterocolitica*.

Vibrio

Vibrio species are prevalent in estuarine and marine environments, and seven species can cause foodborne infections associated with seafood. *Vibrio cholerae* O1 and O139 serovtypes produce cholera toxin and are agents of cholera. However, fecal-oral route infections in the terrestrial environment are responsible for epidemic cholera. *V. cholerae* non-O1/O139 strains may cause gastroenteritis through production of known toxins or unknown mechanism. *Vibrio parahaemolytitcus* strains capable of producing thermostable direct hemolysin (TDH) and/or TDH-related hemolysin are most important causes of gastroenteritis associated with seafood consumption. *Vibrio vulnificus* is responsible for seafoodborne primary septicemia, and its infectivity depends primarily on the risk factors of the host. *V. vulnificus* infection has the highest case fatality rate (50%) of any foodborne pathogen. Four other species (*V. mimicus, V. hollisae, V. fluvialis,* and *V. furnissii*) can cause gastroenteritis. Some strains of these species produce known toxins, but the pathogenic mechanism is largely not understood. The ecology of and detection and control methods for all seafoodborne *Vibrio* pathogens are essentially similar.

Staphylococcus Aureus

Staphylococcus aureus is a common cause of bacterial foodborne disease worldwide. Symptoms include vomiting and diarrhea that occur shortly after ingestion of *S. aureus* toxin-contaminated food.

The symptoms arise from ingestion of preformed enterotoxin, which accounts for the short incubation time. Staphylococcal enterotoxins are superantigens and, as such, have adverse effects on the immune system. The enterotoxin genes are accessory genetic elements in *S. aureus,* meaning not all strains of this organism are enterotoxin-producing.

The enterotoxin genes are found on prophages, plasmids, and pathogenicity islands in different strains of *S. aureus*. Expression of the enterotoxin genes is often under the control of global virulence gene regulatory systems.

Campylobacter

Campylobacter spp., primarily *C. jejuni* subsp. *jejuni* is one of the major causes of bacterial gastroenteritis in the U.S. and worldwide. *Campylobacter* infection is primarily a foodborne illness, usually without complications; however, serious sequelae, such as Guillain-Barre Syndrome, occur in a small subset of infected patients. Detection of *C. jejuni* in clinical samples is readily accomplished by culture and non-culture methods.

Listeria Monocytogenes

Listeria monocytogenes is Gram-positive foodborne bacterial pathogen and the causative agent of human listeriosis. *Listeria* infections are acquired primarily through the consumption of contaminated foods, including soft cheese, raw milk, deli salads, and ready-to-eat foods such as luncheon meats and frankfurters. Although *L. monocytogenes* infection is usually limited to individuals that are immunocompromised, the high mortality rate associated with human listeriosis makes it the leading cause of death among foodborne bacterial pathogens. As a result, tremendous effort has been made to develop methods for the isolation, detection and control of *L. monocytogenes* in foods.

Salmonella

Salmonella serotypes continue to be a prominent threat to food safety worldwide. Infections are commonly acquired by animal to human transmission though consumption of undercooked food products derived from livestock or domestic fowl.

The second half of the 20th century saw the emergence of *Salmonella* serotypes that became associated with new food sources (*i.e.* chicken eggs) and the emergence of *Salmonella* serotypes with resistance against multiple antibiotics.

Shigella

Shigella species are members of the family Enterobacteriaceae and are Gram negative, non-motile rods. Four subgroups exist based on O-antigen structure and biochemical properties: *S. dysenteriae* (subgroup A), *S. flexneri* (subgroup B), *S. boydii* (subgroup C) and *S. sonnei* (subgroup D). Symptoms include mild to severe diarrhea with or without blood, fever, tenesmus and abdominal pain. Further complications of the disease may be seizures, toxic megacolon, reactive arthritis and hemolytic uremic syndrome. Transmission of the pathogen is by the fecal-oral route, commonly through food and water. The infectious dose ranges from 10-100 organisms. *Shigella* spp. have a sophisticated pathogenic mechanism to invade colonic epithelial cells of the host, man and higher primates, and the ability to multiply intracellularly and spread from cell to adjacent cell via actin polymerization. *Shigella* spp. are one of the leading causes of bacterial foodborne illnesses and can spread quickly within a population.

Escherichia coli

More information is available concerning *Escherichia coli* than any other organism, thus making *E. coli* the most thoroughly studied species in the microbial world. For many years, *E. coli* was considered a commensal of human and animal intestinal tracts with low virulence potential.

It is now known that many strains of *E. coli* act as pathogens, inducing serious gastrointestinal diseases and even death in humans. There are six major categories of *E. coli* strains that cause enteric diseases in humans, including the:

1. enterohemorrhagic *E. coli,* which cause haemorrhagic colitis and hemolytic uremic syndrome;
2. enterotoxigenic *E. coli,* which induce traveller's diarrhoea;
3. enteropathogenic *E. coli,* which cause a persistent diarrhoea in children living in developing countries;
4. enteroaggregative *E. coli,* which provokes diarrhoea in children;
5. enteroinvasive *E. coli* that are biochemically and genetically related to *Shigella* species and can induce diarrhoea; and
6. diffusely adherent *E. coli,* which cause diarrhoea and are distinguished by a characteristic type of adherence to mammalian cells.

Clostridium Botulinum and Clostridium Perfringens

Clostridium botulinum produces extremely potent neurotoxins that result in the severe neuroparalytic disease, botulism. The enterotoxin produced by C. *perfringens* during sporulation of vegetative cells in the host intestine results in debilitating acute diarrhea and abdominal pain. Sales of refrigerated, processed foods of extended durability including sous-vide foods, chilled ready-to-eat meals, and cook-chill foods have increased over recent years. Anaerobic spore-formers have been identified as the primary microbiological concerns in these foods.

Heightened awareness over intentional food source tampering with botulinum neurotoxin has arisen with respect to genes encoding the toxins that are capable of transfer to non-toxigenic clostridia.

Bacillus Cereus

The *Bacillus cereus* group comprises six members: *B. anthracis, B. cereus, B. mycoides, B. pseudomycoides, B. thuringiensis* and *B. weihenstephanensis*. These species are closely related and should be placed within one species, except for *B. anthracis* that possesses specific large virulence plasmids. *B. cereus* is a normal soil inhabitant, and is frequently isolated from a variety of foods, including vegetables, dairy products and meat. It causes a vomiting or diarrhoea illness that is becoming increasingly important in the industrialized world.

Some patients may experience both types of illness simultaneously. The diarrhoeal type of illness is most prevalent in the western hemisphere, whereas the emetic type is most prevalent in Japan. Desserts, meat dishes, and dairy products are the foods most frequently associated with diarrhoeal illness, whereas rice and pasta are the most common vehicles of emetic illness.

The emetic toxin (cereulide) has been isolated and characterized; it is a small ring peptide synthesised non-ribosomally by a peptide synthetase. Three types of *B. cereus* enterotoxins involved in foodborne outbreaks have been identified. Two of these enterotoxins are three-component proteins and are related, while the last is a one-component protein (CytK).

Deaths have been recorded both by strains that produce the emetic toxin and by a strain producing only CytK. Some strains of the *B. cereus* group are able to grow at refrigeration temperatures. These variants raise concern about the safety of cooked, refrigerated foods with an extended shelf life. *B. cereus* spores adhere to many surfaces and survive normal washing and disinfection (except for hypochlorite and UVC) procedures. *B. cereus* food borne illness is likely under-reported because of its relatively mild symptoms, which are of short duration.

Food Authenticity

It is important to be able to detect microorganisms in food, in particular pathogenic microorganisms or genetically modified microorganisms. Real-time PCR is an accepted analytical tool within the food industry. Its principal role has been one of assisting the legislative authorities, major manufacturers and retailers to confirm the authenticity of foods. The most obvious role is the detection of genetically modified organisms, but real-time PCR makes a significant contribution to other areas of the food industry, including food safety.

19 Food Preservation Methods

The dictionary meaning of the word 'preserve' is to keep safe, retain quality, prevent decomposition or fermentation. When we apply this meaning to food preservation it can be defined as:

> "A process by which certain foods like fruits and vegetables are prevented from getting spoilt for a long period of time. The colour, taste and nutritive value of the food is also preserved".

Let us understand this definition in a little more detail. The definition says *preventing foods from getting spoilt*. When you keep fruits, vegetables or left over dal in the refrigerator or in a cool place, will this be called food preservation? No, because you can store fruits and vegetables or left over dal in this state for a few days only.

The definition of food preservation states that the preserved food should *retain their colour and taste*. This means that the colour and taste of food which is present at the time of preservation should not change.

Let us take the example of preserving grapesas raisins. Raisins are prepared by sun drying grapes. During the drying process the grapes change colour from green to brown, and taste, sweeter. However, once they are dried and stored, they do not change colour or taste.

Like colour and taste, a well preserved food should *not change texture.* When your mother makes mango murraba at home, have you observed the texture of the mango pieces? It is firm . In a well made murraba, this firmness of mango pieces should not change after sometime.

Why Do We Need to Preserve Foods?

Now that you have understood the definition of food preservation, did you think about why we should preserve foods? Can you think of a few reasons for preserving foods? Let us find an answer to this question by taking an example of one food item.

Let us take the example of a fruit, say mango. There are many ways by which mangoes can be preserved. These are: juice, murraba, squash, aam papad, pulp, chutney, pickle, raw mango powder.

You may be able to add a few more to the above list. Mango is a summer fruit and grows in large quantities during the months of April to August.Different varieties of mango are grown in different parts of our country. Usually all the quantity grown in a region cannot be consumed by the people staying there as there is always an excess. What does the farmer do with this excess quantity? He makes arrangements to transport the excess quantity to regions where either mango is not grown or where that particular variety of mango is not available. If he does not do this, the excess produce will rot and go waste. The farmer will then lose money.

There is still some quantity which is left after the fresh fruit is consumed by the people. It is this quantity which has to be preserved for consumption during the months when mango is not available. Preservation of foods is done during the months when food is available in large quantity and therefore at low cost.

One of the important reasons for preserving foods is to take care ofthe excess produce. There are many other reasons for preserving foods. The second reason for preserving foods is that they add variety to our meals.

Have you ever got tired of eating the same vegetables which are in season? Is it not nice to eat peas when they are either very expensive in the market or are not available? Eating cauliflower in pulav or cauliflower vegetable during the summer months adds to the interest in meals. In the same way, eating some chatni, papad or pickle along with the meals adds to the variety. Preserving foods when they are in season makes this possible.

Reaches Areas where the Food Item is not Grown

In some areas of Rajasthan which are desert areas and in Himalayan regions that are covered with snow most of the time, very few foods can be grown. Availability of some preserved foods can add to the variety and nutritive value of meals. For example inclusion of dehydrated peas, green leafy vegetables, canned fruits etc, in the meals is a good idea in such areas.

Makes Transportation and Storage of Foods Easier

Preservation of foods usually reduces bulk. This makes their transportation and storage easier since it requires less space. For example, if you dry green leafy vegetables such as mint, methi, corriander, etc, their weight and volume reduces, thus making their storage easy.

Why does Food Get Spoilt

The definition of food preservation states that preservation is keeping food in such a state that they do not get spoilt for a long period. Before we look at the reasons of food spoilage, let us understand, when is a food spoilt. When you keep bread outside the refrigerator for few days, a spongy growth is seen on it, which may be white, green on black in colour.

The bread thus gets spoilt due to growth of mold and becomes unfit for consumption. Likewise, if cooked dal or vegetables is left outside for sometime, it develops a bad smell and bubbles due to fermentation. The dal and vegetables are thus spoilt and cannot be eaten. Can you now say when is a food spoilt? Food is said to be spoilt if there is rotting i.e., bad smell, fermentation, bubbles/gas in the food or mold, spongy growth on the food stuff. Formation of soft spots or soft brown spots on fruits and vegetables is also food spoilage.

Why do foods get spoilt? If you know the reasons of food spoilage, you can remove these conditions while preserving food items. Foods get spoilt mainly due to the presence of micro-organisms, enzymes (present in foods), insects, worms, and rats. Let us discuss these factors in some more detail.

1. *Presence of micro-organisms:* Micro means small. Micro-organisms are very small organisms which cannot be easily seen. Micro-organisms spoil food items when the condition for their growth are appropriate. What are these appropriate conditions? Like all living beings micro-organisms require air, moisture, right temperature and food to grow and multiply. The situations which provide appropriate conditions for growth of micro-organisms, can be listed as:

   - Food having high moisture content
   - Air around the food containing micro-organisms
   - Foods kept for a long time at room temperature
   - Skin of fruits and vegetables getting damaged, thus exposing the food to micro-organisms.
   - Foods with low salt, sugar or acid content

   Resulting in spoilage of foods If you want to prevent spoilage of foods by micro organisms, you must remove the conditions mentioned above.

2. *Presence of enzymes:* Enzymes are chemical susbtances found in all plants and animals. Are enzymes harmful to foods? No, enzymes help in ripening of fruits and vegetables. A raw green mango after a few days becomes sweet in taste and yellow in colour due to the enzymes action. What will happen if you keep this yellow, ripe mango for a few more days? It will become soft, develop black spots and will start smelling bad. This is due to

continued action of enzymes. No one likes to eat such as over ripe, spoilt mango. You know that even when the skin of fruits is not cut or damaged, it gets spoilt. This is due to enzyme action.

3. *Insects, worms and rats:* Have you noticed small brownish black insects or small white worms in rice and dals? These insects eat the food grains. They make small holes in the grain and at times convert the grain to a fine powder. The food grain thus become unfit for human consumption.

You have just learnt the three main causes of food spoilage due to micro-organisms, enzymes action and insects, worms and rats.

Principles of Food Preservation

After learning about the causes of food spoilage, it should not be very difficult to list the principles of food preservation. Remember, a good method of food preservation is one that slows down or prevents altogether the action of the agents of spoilage. Also, during the process of food preservation, the food should not be damaged. In order to achieve this, certain basic methods were applied using the knowledge gained form observation of the effects of natural conditions on different types of foods. For example in earlier days, in very cold weather condition, ice was used to preserved foods.

Thus, very low temperature became an efficient method for preventing food spoilage. Let us now list the principles of food preservation.

1. *Removal of micro-organisms or inactivating them:* This is done by removing air, water (moisture), lowering or increasing temperature, increasing the concentration of salt or sugar or acid in foods. If you want to preserve green leafy vegetables, you have to remove the water from the leave so that micro-organisms cannot survive. You do this by drying the green leaves till all the moisture evaporates.
2. *Inactivating enzymes:* Enzymes found in foods can be inactivated by changing their conditions such as temperature and moisture, when you preserve peas, one

of the methods of preservations is to put them for a few minutes in boiling water. This method inactivates enzymes and thus, in preserving the food.

3. *Removal of insects, worms and rats:* By storing foods in dry, air tight containers the insects, worms or rats are prevented from destroying it.

Methods of Preserving Foods at Home

Foods can be preserved at home by the following methods:

1. Dehydration
2. Lowering temperature
3. Increasing temperature
4. Using preservatives

Let us now discuss each method in some detail.

Dehydration

Can you name some dried food items that are stored in your kitchen for a period of one year or more? Are these potato chips, sevia (vermicilli), methi, cauliflower, papad, ginger powder? These are foods which have been preserved by the dehydration method. The word dehydration means removing water or moisture from foods. The home method of dehydration is sun drying. We will now discuss this method in some more detail.

Some foods are dried as they are, *e.g.*, green leafy vegetables (methi, pudina, corriander etc.) cauliflower, grapes, amla, onion, raw mango, etc. Some foods are cooked and then dried. For example potato chips, papad, banana, chips, wadis, etc. The most appropriate weather to dry foods is when the air is dry and there is strong sunshine. Let us understand the basic method of dehydration before we learn to apply it to individual foods.

Step–1: Clean all tins, plates, etc, to be used to dry and store the food. Dry in sun. Storage tins should have airtight lids.

Step–2: Wash the vegetables/fruits to be dehydrated. Cut, if required. Remove the stem, seeds, skin. Remove any decaying portions.

Step–3: Blanch vegetables, i.e., put them in boiling water. Time for blanching varies with hardness of fruit/vegetables. Remove when the food is soft (blanching reduces enzymed activity).

Step–4: Put vegetables in cold water containing salt and potassium.

Food Preservation: 73 metabisulphite(kms) for 5-10 minutes. This prevents blackening of foods. Green leafy vegetables and other dark vegetables should not be put in this solution.

Step–5: Spread on a clean cloth in the sun. Cover with a thin cloth to avoid dust and flies getting into the food.

Step–6: When the food is dry, (test by looking at hardness), cool to room temperature. Store in an air tight container. When you want to use dehydrated fruits and vegetables, wash and soak in water for some time. Now let us look at how you can use this method to preserve a specific food items, eg, methi and potato.

Dehydrating Methi

Can you list the steps for drying methi?

1. Wash methi and remove the stems.
2. Put on a cloth in the sun, cover it.
3. Cool to room temperature and store in air tight tins.

Making Potato Chips

1. Wash and peel potatoes. Cut in thin round slices.
2. Put in boiling water for 3-4 minutes.
3. Make a solution in cold water with 4 tsp salt, ¾ tsp potassium metabisulphite (for 4 kg potato).
4. Put the blanched potato chips in this solution for 10 minutes.
5. Spread each chip separately on a plate in the sun. Cover with a thin cloth.
6. When dry, cool and store in air tight containers.

So, even if the basic principle of dehydration remains the same, you have to adapt the method depending on the food you are preserving.

Lowering Temperature

Using low temperature to preserve foods works on the principle that low temperature slows microbial and enzyme action. The food is thus prevented from spoilage. Are you using this method of preservation at home? Yes, if you have a refrigerator you can use it because a refrigerator works on this principle. Foods can be preserved at low temperature by:

1. Refrigeration 40ºC to 70ºC
2. Cold storage – 10ºC to – 40ºC
3. Freezing –180ºC or below

The duration for which the food can be preserved by using low temperature varies with the type of food and the temperatures. The lower the temperature, longer is the duration for which food can be preserved. Of the three methods, freezing uses the lowest temperature.

Since cold storage and freezing are both not used very commonly at home as methods of preservation, we will not discuss the details in this section. You have already learnt about refrigeration in a previous lesson.

Freezing Method

Step–1: Select about half a kilogram of fresh, tender peas and shell them.

Step–2: Take enough water in a stainless steel pan in which the peas can be completely immersed. Add 1 teaspoon of salt for half litre of water, dissolve and bring the solution to boil.

Step–3: Completely immerse the peas in the boiling solution for about 2 minutes.

Step–4: Drain the peas immediately on to a stainless steel sieve and let it cool for 10-15 minutes.

Step–5: Pack the peas in polythene bags, remove the air by pressing and seal the bags.

Step–6: Put the packets of peas into a freezer.

Note: Similarly other vegetables such as cauliflower, beans, carrots etc can also be frozen.

Using Frozen Vegetables

1. Take out the frozen packet from the freezer one and a half hours or two hours before use and let it thaw to room temperature. Put peas in a sieve and keep under tap water for a few minutes. Drain and use.
2. Frozen vegetables can be stored up to six months in a freezer.

Precautions while Freezing Fruits and Vegetables

1. Packaging material, that is, polythene bags should be strong enough to withstand expansion of food material on freezing. The food once brought out of the freezer and up to room temperature should not be refrozen.
2. Small packets should be prepared, as food once thawed must be consumed. So there is less chance of the unrequired food material being spoilt. This also helps to avoid refreezing of the unutilized food material.
3. Exclude the air carefully and completely from the package before sealing.
4. The freezer should not be opened too frequently.

Thaw: A process by which something frozen is brought to room temperature without applying artificial heat.

Increasing Temperature

By increasing the temperature, enzymes and micro organisms are destroyed, leaving the food safe from spoilage. Do all organisms get killed by increasing temperature? No, there are some micro-organisms which do not get destroyed at high temperature. If these organisms are not killed, they can spoil food items once the temperature is lowered. There are mainly two methods of preserving foods by using high temperature:

1. *Pasteurization:* When you think of pasteurization, which food item comes to your mind? Yes, its milk. We have often heard about pasteurized milk packets. In this method food is heated to a high temperature and then quickly cooled. The micro-organisms are not able to withstand the sudden change in temperature and are destroyed. However, some organisms still survive this method.
2. *Sterilization:* What does the word sterilization mean? It means free from any living organism. The high temperature used in this method destroys all the micro-organisms in the food. The foods are exposed to high temperature for longer time and in some cases under pressure. When a pressure cooker is used to cook, the food lasts longer because most micro-organisms get destroyed. You can also sterilize bottles and other equipments used in preservation.

Using Preservatives

What are preservatives? Any substance that is added to foods to make it last for a longer time is called a preservative. You have learnt that increasing the concentration of salt, sugar or acid in a food prevents its spoilage. Therefore, salt, sugar or acid are substances which act as preservatives. There are two types of preservatives:

1. *Natural Preservatives:* Salt, sugar, lemon juice, vinegar, oil and spices are natural preservatives.
2. *Chemical preservatives:* Potassium metabisulphate, citric acid and sodium benzoate are chemical preservatives.

   Let us discuss the natural preservatives.

(a) *Salt:* When you make pickle at home, salt is one of the ingredients used. Did you think that salt is added only for taste? Besides adding to taste, salt has a specific function, *i.e.,* to act as a preservative. If the proportion of salt in pickles is less, it can get spoilt after sometime.

   How does salt act as a preservative? Increasing the quantity of salt in the food changes its composition. Due to the presence of salt in the food, osmosis takes place. As a result, water comes out of the food. When there is no or less water in the food, the micro-organisms are not able to grow and the food becomes safe. Salt also reduces the activity of enzymes, thus preventing the food from getting spoilt. Salt is used as a preservative in pickles, chatni, sauce, canned food, etc. Salt is rubbed on fish which helps to preserve it.

(b) *Sugar:* Can you think of some preserved foods where sugar is used as a preservative? Yes, these are jams, jellies, murabbas, squashes. Like in pickle, chatni, etc., sugar is added to these foods not only for taste but also as a preservative.

The proportion of sugar has to be correct to protect them from spoiling. How does sugar prevent food spoilage? The sugar dissolves in the water availFood able in the food item. This results in less water being available for the growth of micro-organisms. Hence the food becomes safe.

(c) *Acids:* Can you think of any sour food items used as preservative? These are lemon juice, vinegar, citric acid, etc. Vinegar is used to preserve onions, tomato ketchup; lemon juice is used in pickles; citric acid is used in squashes. Acids increase the acidic content of food items, thus preventing the activity and growth of micro-organisms.

(d) *Oils and spices:* These are used as preservatives in pickles. Can you think of a spice which is commonly used as a preservatives? Yes, mustard powder is one of them. It prevents the growth of micro organisms, thus preventing spoilage. When pickle is made at home, have you observed that oil is poured to cover the mango, lemon or other vegetables which are being pickled. The oil acts as a protective cover and has two advantages:

1. prevents contact of micro-organisms with the food, hence they can not spoil the food.

2. prevents contact of air with food, hence the micro organisms can not grow and spoil the food. You have learnt some of the common methods of food preservation. Generally, a combination of the principles of preservation is used. For example, in pickles you use large amounts of salt, spices and oil. In the same way, acids and a lot of sugar are used for making squashes.

1. **Use of Natural Preservative**
   - Method of making jam
   - Apple Jam
   - Ingrdients:
   - Apples: 1 kg
   - Sugar: 750 gms
   - Citric Acid: 1 teaspoon
   - Water: 250 ml

Method

Step–1: Select firm apples and wash them thoroughly by rubbing them clean.

Step–2: Cut them into small pieces. While cutting remove the core and hard seeds, but do not remove skin or peel.

Step–3: Cook in water till apple pieces are tender. (you can also pressure cook them for 1 whistle only.)

Step–4: Sieve the pulp carefully.

Step–5: Add sugar and citric acid with constant stirring.

Step–6: Cook till the mixture has done the plate test.

Step–7: Pour hot jam into wide mouthed, sterilized bottles and cool.

Step–8: Store in a cool place.

Plate Test: Put a spoonful of the cooked mixture on a plate. Let it cool slightly. Tilt the plate. If the jam is ready, the mass moves together as a lump. If liquid separates and pulp remains, it needs more cooking.

2. Use of Chemical Preservatives

- ❖ Orange Squash
- ❖ Ingredients
- ❖ Orange juice: 1 litre
- ❖ Sugar: 2 kgs.
- ❖ Water: 1 litre
- ❖ Potassium Metabisulphite: Half teaspoon
- ❖ Orange Essence: 1 teaspoon
- ❖ Citric Acid: 30 gms

Method

Step–1: Squashes are prepared from juicy fruits. Select juicy oranges and extract the juice.

Step–2: Take water, sugar and citric and boil the mixture till the sugar is completely dissolved.

Step–3: Add orange colour, essence and juice.

Step–4: Dissolve the potassium metabisulphite in a little juice and mix it into the prepared squash.

Step–5: Pour it into sterilized bottles. Seal it or close it tightly.

Step–6: Store the bottles in a cool place and away from the sun.

Some Useful Tips

Let us discuss some tips which will be useful for taking care of the preserved food items.

1. Take care of hygiene while preparing the food and storing it. The utensils and containers used to cook and store food items should be thoroughly cleaned and dried in sun. The containers should have air tight lids.
2. While preserving pickles take care that a layer of oil is above the vegetables, so that these do not come in contact with the air.
3. While using the preserved food items, take care to use clean spoons. Close the lid immediately after removing the required quantity.

4. For foods like sauces and squashes, the bottles should be sterilized and kept in hot water till they are needed. You could first put the preserved food in the bottles and then sterilize the bottles by heating them in water for 30-40 minutes.

References

Riddervold, Astri. *Food Conservation*. ISBN 978-09-0732-540-6.

Hauther,W. & Worth, M., Zapped! Irradiation and the Death of Food, Food & Water Watch Press, Washington, DC, 2008.

Annis, P.C. and Morton, R. 1997. The Acute Mortality Effects of Carbon Dioxide on Various Life Stages of Sitophilus Oryzae. J. Stored Prod.Res. 33. 115-124.

Alzamora SM, Tapia MS and López-Malo A (2000) *Minimally Processed Fruits and Vegetables: Fundamental Aspects and Applications* Springer, p. 266. ISBN 978-08-3421-672-3.

Levenstein, H: "Paradox of Plenty", pp. 106-107. University of California Press, 2003.

Laudan, Rachel (September/October 2010). "In Praise of Fast Food". UTNE Reader. http://www.utne.com/Environment/Fast-Food-Culinary-Ethos.aspx? p.4. Retrieved 2010-09-24. "Where Modern Food Became Available, People Grew Taller and Stronger and Lived Longer."

Laudan, Rachel (September/October 2010). "In Praise of Fast Food". UTNE Reader. http://www.utne.com/Environment/Fast-Food-Culinary-Ethos.aspx? p. 4. Retrieved 2010-09-24. "If we Fail to Understand how Scant and Monotonous Most Traditional Diets Were, We Can

Misunderstand the "Ethnic Foods" we Encounter in Cookbooks, at Restaurants, or on Our Travels".

Laudan, Rachel (September/October 2010). "In Praise of Fast Food". Retrieved 2010-09-24. "For Our Ancestors, Natural was Something Quite Nasty. Natural Often Tasted Bad. Fresh Meat was Rank and Tough, Fresh Fruits Inedibly Sour, Fresh Vegetables Bitter".

Laudan, Rachel (September/October 2010). "In Praise of Fast Food". UTNE Reader. http://www.utne.com/Environment/Fast-Food-Culinary-Ethos.aspx? p. 4. Retrieved 2010-09-24.

Pollan, Michael (2008). *In Defense of Food: An Eater's Manifesto*. New York, USA: Penguin Press. ISBN 978-15-9420-145-5.

Fennema, O.R., Ed. (1985). *Food Chemistry — Second Edition, Revised and Expanded*. New York: Marcel Dekker, Inc.

Francis, F.J. (2000). "Harvey W. Wiley: Pioneer in Food Science and Quality." In *A Century of Food Science*. Chicago: Institute of Food Technologists. pp. 13-14.

Potter, N.N. and J.H. Hotchkiss. (1995). *Food Science, Fifth Edition*. New York: Champman & Hall. pp. 24-68.

U.S. Food and Drug Administration. (1993). *Everything Added to Food in the United States*. Boca Raton, FL: C.K. Smoley (c/o CRC Press, Inc.).

Food Control, ISSN: 0956-7135, Elsevier.

Journal of Food Protection, ISSN 0362-028X, International Association for Food Protection.

Sensing and Instrumentation for Food Quality and Safety, ISSN: 1932-9954 (electronic) ISSN: 1932-7587 (paper), Springer.

Internet Journal of Food Safety, ISSN: 1930-0670, International Association for Food Safety/Quality.

Mark Clute (October 2008). *Food Industry Quality Control Systems*. [CRC Press]. ISBN 978-0-8493-8028-0.

Index